ODYSSEY

Through Nooks of Life in
Parts of Nagaland and Manipur

SUSHANT
MALLIK

INDIA · SINGAPORE · MALAYSIA

Notion Press

Old No. 38, New No. 6
McNichols Road, Chetpet
Chennai - 600 031

First Published by Notion Press 2019
Copyright © Sushant Mallik 2019
All Rights Reserved.

ISBN 978-1-64587-287-0

Disclaimer

A ll the characters and names adopted in this work of fiction are imaginary and any sort of resemblance to any fact or part of life with any name so adopted or any individual is purely unintentional and coincidental. Names of some specific locations or villages are also used with no ill intention and solely to make all the events realistic.

Contents

Contents

Acknowledgement

I convey my heartfelt gratitude to my family members for all their support. Special thanks to Jayanta Maitra M.A., B.Ed., my close friend, to take pain for initial editing and suggesting the befitting name of the book as initially I thought to have the title of the book as "The Voyage".

My honest compliments to all concerned officials of Notion Press for their consistent and necessary guidance and encouragement to get the book ready for publishing.

Illustrations have been illuminated by Dr Abhishek Mallik and Sushant Mallik.

Prologue

::

My stay from 1992 to 1998 in Nagaland and Manipur was full of learning and a true revelation for me. There might have been a lot of changes after that, but I was certainly privileged to experience the golden essence of life in the Northeast. So time taken to make all such facts, that I came across, to get shaped in black and white may cause the language, description or course of events a bit out of place in today's perspective. At times, I had to face some grievous and challenging situations but local villagers always supported me greatly.

I take the opportunity to share the experience of my voyage through the huge sea of humanity in Northeastern India. It may not sound like we are talking about pearls but pebbles. But pearls are momentary and serve a few as valuables, whereas pebbles are invaluable and consistent with nature. I always take every care to pick up eye-soothing pebbles enroute. Visiting remote villages in the Northeast is really venturing to the abode of God. It is people's faith in God that enables them to have the strength to live a happy life despite being very far from reaching amenities.

Different tribes are like different flowers as created by God in this beautiful terrain.

The book is an effort to invite attention to a few rustic and unconventional happenings in a certain corner of India which remains less talked about.

Finally it is all inspiration and encouragement from every member of my family and friends, and the sense of gratitude all my learning from those people that made me take up the pen despite a heavy work load, and start writing by utilising all short or shorter respites. And once I started, it has consequently turned to be quite complacent.

1. Quest for Destiny

For human beings life is nothing but a journey in the quest for destiny, which is purely our aim or goal. For most of us, the journey of life or the very quest ends before we could actually reach the destiny. Perhaps, reaching there is not in our hands or disposal, as our destiny has always been predestined by the ultimate disposer. Unless you are destined, you cannot achieve your goal. So, in every new lap of our journey to our desired goal we should pat ourselves for reaching that much, because tomorrow, as we know, is only an irrefutable (as well as expected) illusion. But we must be prepared for tomorrow and that is actually what life is! Preparing ourselves for facing the unknown but imminent challenges, irrespective of our status or support behind us, is called living; no matter whether one is privileged or not, to have guidance or support to keep on living or moving forward to reach that destiny. Our journey may make us, at times, to come across the master, the guru or the guide on the way to inspire us to do the right thing in the right way. There is no dearth of teachers around us. So I never stopped striding forward, undermining present silly situations that may appear as hindrances. I am lucky that I always have my conscience to stand by me and help me to make the right decisions, the most precious provision for the journey of life. So I find living actually as moving forward.

Except enlightenment gathered from books or maps, my idea of India and her people was quite fictitious because I never had any opportunity to trip to any significant place even at some distance from my home. But, I believe I was fairly good, or better, in map pointing or to pen down the sketch of people from any particular part of India or even that of the world. I loved to dream about an India that would not have the least resemblance with India in reality.

I hardly had any occasion to come out of my hometown. I hardly stayed for a few days out of my home except in some rare exigency. So it was of immense pleasure for me to discover India and the world in books or newspapers. By the time I entered class sixth or seventh, I visited almost all the prominent places under the sky a number of times by riding on the words, sentences or expression in various books. I used to be engaged for hours by thinking about the place or roaming in and around that place about which I read a few lines in any book, magazine or paper. It was nothing but a sort of reverie due to my sincere wish to step into those very places. I ventured with Eskimos in their sledges and stayed with them in their Igloos. Sometimes I enjoyed a safari in the deepest African forest. Nobody could resist me either in passing days in islands, in the Andaman and Nicobar, with Jarwa or watching the mummies and huge treasures by sneaking into the Pyramids. I even travelled to outer space with Flash Gordon or Tintin.

So to some extent I was a global citizen. For me, Delhi was as far as Washington or Tokyo was. We used to wallow in the little pond in our locality swimming for hours but it was not less than going in to the centre of Bermuda Triangle in those days of sincere innocence. Dreams were endless and so was my zeal. It was great being on the wings of imagination and watching the known world from high in the firmament, and then come back again before the dark set in.

I had always been surrounded by caring elders and good friends in a homogeneous and supportive society. Hence, hardship all around could never get better of my consistency to follow the right path. I grew up by nurturing my wish to work for the people, and for the needy in particular. Like other friends of our group, I never minded working more and more or to sacrifice leisure or sleep for the cause of society or humankind. I always love to inspire myself by quotes from Robert Bierstedt *"I am not what I think I am, and I am not what you think I am. I am what I think you think I am"*.

Fortunately, I got a central government job to work for needy people by staying within or near them. I did not have any foreknowledge about the nature of the task I was to be entrusted with but gradually, I discovered, with good grace that it was actually the work for which I was always ready to volunteer myself. So it was a dream job for me. It appeared that I was actually being paid for the fruition of my long cherished dream. I was lucky that I was given the opportunity to know India, specially a less-known side of India, and to realise the unique diversities of this country.

It is of real bliss for me that I am considered to start my journey for discovering India from the remotest parts of Nagaland, Manipur and other Northeastern states where the sunrays touch the land in the morning to shower energy before reaching any other part of India. I am proud of the diverse cultural characteristics of our country and I respect that emblem of our democracy which led all different creeds, cultures, faith, believe, customs or identity to work together for the triumph of humanity despite all furtive effort to harm the spirit of our sovereignty. Learning all such essence is learning about true nationalism, as I understood.

For my friends and me, a single afternoon in the playground was too short to enjoy various types of games entirely. In most of those afternoons we used to be busy with at least two to three games out of football, cricket, volleyball or kabaddi and many others, though most of us were about to complete or had already completed our college. That playground was indeed the only place where we could reduce our agony, hardship, tension or pain for being jobless or visionless, and where we could yield the zeal to cope with the materialistic and insensitive world by sharing all our zest with its compassionate grass and earth in the pretext of playing.

One afternoon, I was playing cricket with my daring friends after completing a long course of football match among us wishing the charming afternoon dare not to allow the darkness of the evening to set its foot on earth. At that auspicious moment, my little brother came rushing in to the ground and shouted, "Dada, letter. The peon is waiting. It is a registered letter. It seems urgent".

I came home in that seemingly odd hour. I thought it might be a call letter for one more interview or recruitment test as in those days we used to be busy appearing for such tests in all most every week or month. So I opened the envelope without any reluctance. But it was a different one. I went through that; I went through the lines and between the lines twice, thrice and more. It was really an appointment letter. Yes, it was that! My heart popped up with a flicker of dubiety. The authority wanted me to join immediately at Imphal for the job for which I had appeared for physical, written and viva test months back.

I became a helpless subject of time after that. Time did not allow me to have more time; neither was I spared to have any other option than to join the job. I knew Imphal, a beautiful city and the capital of Manipur, was near to the mysterious and beautiful Loktak Lake. As I read in some book, Manipur was to be the land of great warriors and it was the land of 'Chitrangada'. I did not know more than that. I was badly in need of a job.

Moreover, I came to know that like me, people in Imphal too are fond of 'bhaat' or rice, the most delicious white blessing of God. I came to know people were honest and friendly there. So, I decided to set out for Imphal.

Time flied fast. A feast was arranged by all my friends to bid me adieu with an admixture of tears and smiles. It was immensely tortuous for me that I was going to miss all my friends. That time I realised how crude it was to go away from friends who were so special to me. They knew me more than I knew myself. It was very difficult for me to leave my family behind. But time being the most ruthless teacher, dragged me out at the railway station with my belongings. My family and my friends came to see me off with their ardent and honest affection. For me, it was indeed the strongest support.

All tried their best to boost me up and instil a tinge of confidence at that crux moment. But when my mother started weeping with the blowing of the train whistle, tears splashed in all the eyes. I too was in tears as the train started trailing out of the platform. I did not know how long I stood beside the door looking outside with a fuzzy fantasy. I was driven away from the station and from my native and its soil from where I had never ever imagined to be away for even a few days. After a few seconds, the station was out of my sight. I was alone among the many passengers in that compartment. For a long time, I did not stare at any of the co-passengers. In fact, initially I was very angry that God had compelled me to leave my native place in such a ruthless way. After sometime, after some argument with Him in my mind, I conceded that I should thank God for rendering me a boon in the shape of a job. I apologised and thanked Him from the core of my heart. I realised that I was blessed and lucky that I at least got a job to support my family. It gave me profound happiness. I looked forward to it. I watched the beautiful agricultural land, paddy field, small villages, rivers, some towns, stations and everything there in the verdant nature, on the other side of the window, rushing backwards fast. I discovered a rejuvenated me striding forward fast defeating many hard times of mine to know India in a better way by seeing through my own eyes.

I realised that I was actually rushing fast to see and feel the pulse of my India for the first time by going beyond the pages of books. I was confident that by and large 'India in reality' will be almost closer to that India about which I cherished a special dream, be it day or night. Nonetheless, the India of my dream is always a land where every family has a house, a minimum space and befitting work to earn sufficiently to feed their family members, where there is respect for every profession and people hate to live on alms. People are proud of their nationalism and rationally respectful to others religious and national identity, where people are helpful, courteous and courageous to forgive. Above all, people are extremely passionate about preserving the greenery and a healthy environment.

Above all, transcending everything and all exception, a sense of confidence got into my innerself that the job will help me to touch all my dreams. I knew dreaming costs nothing. I knew dreams could help one to fly high, higher or the highest. I knew that I couldbe wrong. But I also knew that even the high flying bird becomes eager to come down to the ground or its nest at the end of the day or at the end of the venture. Dreaming cannot be perpetual.

2.   On the Way to Imphal

It was my first time going out of my home state
alone. Every station was a step forward towards my
destination Imphal. I was spellbound by seeing the majestic
'Brahmaputra' river before heading to Guwahati city. It was
so large and beautiful with some small hillocks raising their
green heads from the river water that I became speechless.
Following most of the fellow passengers, I threw two or
three coins into the river water through the window, praying
nothing. Most of them started worshipping keeping their
hands folded on their chest. Guwahati, a proud abode of
a number of small green hillocks decorated with beautiful
houses in various colours and a lively crowd and traffic
in both the side of the railway track entranced me. It was
pathetic to find a slumberous slum on either sides of the
railway track before getting into the Guwahati railway
station, like at all other major railway stations, where men,
women, their kids, their pigs, their pets were accommodated
in a hut as big as a bed made of plastic sheets or thatch
among heaps of garbage, bottles and filthy mud. However,
I was confident that India would definitely rise one day
from those slums.

The train reached the busy Guwahati railway station with royal idleness. I had never seen so many army or paramilitary personnel with live arms roaming actively almost everywhere as I saw at the Guwahati railway station. I was a bit scared that somewhere war might have started. From every corner emanated the jingling of arms. Starting from Guwahati up to Imphal, I came across the sentinels with heavy arms in trains, in buses, on the road or in the form of convoys several times.

That was the first time I reached Guwahati for further journey to Dimapur and that was the first and the last time I availed the train for reaching Dimapur from Guwahati. It was an overnight journey and I did not like the journey with passengers over cautious about everything around, scared, afraid, and not sleeping at night in a seemingly needless artificial and tense atmosphere. I figured that the political situation along with the activities of various extremist groups was responsible for such a sense of insecurity among general people.

Somehow, I reached Dimapur early in the morning. To me the Dimapur town seemed busy since before dawn. People on foot, on cycle or rickshaw or other vehicles were found restless. As I never like readymade tea, I moved around restlessly and got fresh, hot and smoky tea of my test. Then after rigorous effort, I could manage to locate the bus stop and get a bus heading for Imphal. It was a mail-express bus of the Manipur State Transport. The red coloured bus did not look fit to take so many passengers to such a long distance. But the driver was appropriate. I liked the big-ballooned horn, which sounded 'bhom ...

bhom' scaring and irritating the passer by. I found all those irritated faces to turn into gaiety after a moment and to exchange smiles with the driver. So we proceeded further 'bhom ... bhom'.

That MST bus was full to every inch. Almost all passengers were Manipuri except a few non-Manipuries seated at the back. I could have exchanged my thought in unpolished English or Hindi, but nobody except the conductor talked to me. So I continued talking with the scenic beauty of nature of Nagaland and then Manipur with my eyes. I had never been so close to such beautiful hills, forests, rivers, streams or roadside vegetable shops or teashops, unknown villagers in different types of attire, talking different languages for so long. And for that long period I remained almost hypnotised by everything in my sight on either side of the road, green hill affront, the blue sky above. Everything was so fresh and soothing.

Though I knew that I left my home, my family or my friends for my job, but for how long? I did not have any idea, even then that extreme beauty of nature, seemingly created by the Almighty with all love and care did not let me divert my sight or be dissolved in any sort of gloom. After crossing Dimapur town, the road took us to near the green hill all of a sudden. The bus started going upwards through that curved road. It was high and a higher hill covered with deep green forests all around. It was amazing to see new chains of hills after every turning.

We took tea at a small rural bus stop called Zubza, hosting a few shops for fresh local vegetables, paan, cigarettes, gutka etc, on the sky-high hill. From there the river down at the foothill looked like a flying fillet. I saw a hanging bridge across the river a few minutes back, on which two men, with a load on their back were walking, almost leaping up and down on the toppling floor. The number of streams coming down from the steep hill with wildly dancing water passing over the road by overflowing the drainage was in abundance.

I enjoyed hot tea with some unnamed biscuits. The shopkeeper, a young lady, was politely attending all. She never asked anybody for payment. She was confident that everybody will pay. I found earning that much confidence from an unknown person was a matter of great respect for anybody. I realised that it was normal practice there, just like in the India of my dream. People were found picking up vegetables of their choice from the baskets and searching for the shopkeepers for making the payments. All of a sudden, there was a flush of drizzle for two or three minutes to make the moment more amorous. Most of us did not mind getting wet under that happy rain coming down softly from the nearly clear sky.

After about one hour, the picturesque feature of the cluster of colourful buildings in the background of green hills came into my sight. I remained speechless. It was so beautiful and so large. It was the mighty Kohima. The city was extended throughout more than four or five different hillocks. It was a bright day there. Bright green trees and the conglomeration of vibrant houses along the hilly slope starting from the foothill up to the highest ridge under the azure horizon were mesmerising for me.

It was a tough exercise for me to look at all directions through the window glass to have a glimpse of the city. My co-passenger might have thought my apparent restlessness a bit queer if not at all a stupidity. I could not guess when we entered into the city. Our bus came near the war cemetery. Some of the passengers alighted there. I tried to convince myself that I had really reached Kohima after crossing Guwahati for the first time in my life. I could point out these places on the map easily in my schooldays; I came to know a few details about Nagaland and about Kohima from books.

I found the road full of cars and the footpaths full of pedestrians on their fast move towards workplaces, some people selling cucumbers, peach or roasted corn or sweet potatoes on the same. Some temporary stalls for vegetables, woollen clothes or footwear were also there. For a little eye-to-eye contact, in some incautious moment, I was being greeted with a genuine smile from the other end, as if we knew each other. Those smiles gradually shook away all my diffidence to exchange a smile even with strangers. Western music, local or Hindi songs were being played from the roadside shops at full volume. It was charming. I enjoyed crunching at roasted corn there, it was sweet, and it tasted different for it was from the local village, not pampered by using any artificial manure.

I wanted to visit the cemetery but the bus was to proceed further for Imphal. After a few minutes, we reached at Mao, from where we actually entered into Manipur from Nagaland. Mao-gate was also found to be a busy market. As the bus stopped there, passengers got down quickly and rushed to the nearby stalls for purchasing fresh vegetables or other eatables. The scent of fermented edibles pervaded the air there. It was absolutely new to me. It was different, but also appetising. I came to know it was the smell of fermented bamboo-root.

Passengers came back happily after a short shopping and we started our journey again for the capital of Manipur. After that, there came many other bus-stops on our way such as Tadoubi, Karong or Senapati. Some passengers left the bus at their destination and many others were added to our number. After a little long, at a stoppage named 'Sekmai', I found that all the passengers got down and I was the only passenger left in the bus. The conductor told me in broken Hindi that I could have food there.

I was really hungry as I had finished the 'paratha' and 'alu-dum' packed in a tiffin-box from home the previous night near Guwahati for dinner and I took only a few cups of tea or snacks on the way till I reached 'Sekmai'. I found many buses and other vehicles parked in front of different hut-styled hotels, which did not look like hotels but exactly like neat and clean rural house compounds of well to do farmers. There was no sign of the least dirtiness anywhere in front of or inside any of those house-hotels. Every compound was nicely smeared with mud mixed with cow dung or cement coloured mud. I discovered that most of those hotels were actually house-cum-hotels and the backyard of the main house was attached with a small fishery that was full of fishes, and a small garden for vegetables. It was beyond my imagination, it was just like a well-groomed village. I was not actually able to decide which hotel to go for food. Somehow, I stopped assessing those hotels and took a seat in a less crowded one. It was so neat and clean as if I was in any temple. A gentle man in white dhoti, white half-sleeve kurta and gamchha, with long chandan-tika on his forehead and arms came to me for my order. As I saw everyone else devouring rice, I tried to convey to him that I would like to have rice and fish. One lady, in the typical style of Manipuri sari or mekhla with chandan-tika, just like Vaishnavas came with the food in steel utensils. Those dishes, bowls or glasses were so clean and shining that anybody could be impressed and loved to eat in that homely atmosphere. That was my first meal out of my home state and it was a really grand and unforgettable occasion for me. I was served daal, chatni, green vegetables and fish curry and every preparation was superb. In that chatni I got the scent of fermented bamboo-shoot which I had come across at Mao-gate. I tasted the chatni made of dried-fish, bamboo-shoot and chilly etc, for the first time, and I liked it.

When I asked for lemon, the lady rushed to the garden at once and brought fresh lemons and green-chillies, and gave the sliced lemon and chilly in a small plate happily. So, I took that meal with immense pleasure as if I were eating at my home. The flavour of the local rice was unbelievably appetising, sticky and sweet. I should confess that I ate there with in relish. I was given extra 'chaak' (rice in Manipuri) more than thrice. Beside food, I loved the pious essence of the atmosphere.

Later on, I was told that the very place, namely 'Sekmai', was famous for traditional Manipuri dishes. Besides, that place was also famous and a favourite among people for the kind of liquor, locally made and famous in the name of the place itself, i.e. 'Sekmai'. But I will forever consider that place as one of my most favourite destination for eateries not only for its delicious food but also for its most hospitable hosts or hoteliers. That day onwards I used to travel, rather I preferred to travel, to and from Imphal via Sekmai, time and again, so that I could have food at Sekmai.

Then again, we were in that same bus heading towards Imphal. The hilly track was almost ended. We crossed the last chain of hills which stood as a natural wall to encircle Imphal valley. From that point, the tough hilly track starting from near Dimapur up to Senapati was found changed into a fair road on a plain all of a sudden. We entered the plain region of the valley, leaving so many villages, fisheries, forests, greeneries, markets behind on either side of the road. I never even realised how and when the journey through the hilly terrain lodged us into the valley and lively hubbub of the city life of Imphal.

3.

Capital of Manipur, the Agile Valley

A t about 4 pm I reached Imphal city. The sun was idly going down and the essence of the evening was about to set in. I could not believe that a very domestic being like me actually touched three State-capitals of India within almost 12 hours. I got down at the last stoppage at BOC corner of Imphal. The bus conductor helped me to get to one hotel, namely 'Hotel Tampha', opposite a twin theatre 'Asha-Jina'. I was yet to look for the place and the office where I was to join my duty. I enquired about the location of our office and roamed around all evening as a free man away from home and family. I realised that being free was actually taking more responsibility upon oneself. No known voice was around to remind me about life's dos and don'ts. Hence, it seemed very important for one to have a wise and bold brain which can guide to be good or safe and pat for the good-deeds like guardians.

I again enjoyed a Manipuri dish consisting of chicken at dinner that evening and slept the deepest that night, as the next day happened to be Sunday. I left the hotel early the next morning and had a brisk walk along the major roads to roam around a huge portion of the beautiful city. I visited the polo-ground, the Imma market area and then went up to Lamphelpat. On my very first morning in Imphal, I witnessed the city to wake up. It was amazing to see health conscious people jogging or running on the road, in the playground or at the yard. Police-force personnel were busy in the morning exercise at the polo-ground. Then people on the back of horses were playing polo there. I watched them playing polo for long as it was for the first time that I found people playing polo not on the screen. It was really a tough game. I found children practising martial arts. Some kids were practising lawn tennis by using the wall of their house as the net. They were trying hard to hit the ball properly after it was being struck back by the wall.

I got at least four or five groups of people with 'khol' (a traditional tomtom or drum) and 'kartaal' (brass made cymbals) in procession singing 'kirtana'. They were 'Vaishnavites' – the disciples of Lord Krishna, I could follow only "Harey Krishna, Harey Krishna…" from what they were singing. That morning, the first morning for me at Imphal, turned out to be a real gift. For me it was hard to believe that I really walked for almost three hours that morning and had a glance at the awakening of life in the far east of India far away from my home.

From Lamphelpat, I returned to my hotel following the same route, which was crowded by that time, due to movements of the city dwellers, shoppers, vehicles, rickshaws or cycles. It was a hot day. I returned to the room exhausted. In the noon, as I had nothing to do, I went to 'Asha-Jina' theatre, two movie halls in the same theatre house on the other side of the road and watched a movie, namely 'The Foreign Body' with Victor Banerjee in the lead-role, in 'Asha' theatre in the matinee show. It was a nice movie about how an Indian doctor won the hearts of people abroad. I came out of the hall after the movie was over and drank tea. I neither had anything to convey to any one nor anything to listen from anybody, for I did not know the Manipuri language. I went to the theatre again and watched another movie, namely 'Home Alone' in the evening show at 'Jina' hall. I had never ever thought of watching two movies in a single day. In that way, I did not allow the day to be too long and succeeded in fighting that episode of 'Away Alone' of my life by watching "Foreign Body" and "Home Alone".

At that time, there was a total ban on showing Hindi movies in theatres in Manipur imposed by some underground outfit, though I found many local boys or girls sing popular Hindi songs with passion and in the perfect rhythm. Be it in singing or in playing instruments, they were the masters. The traditional music-troupe, equipped mainly with harmonium, flute and khol, was as popular as the western band.

Soon after evening, the streets around used to be almost deserted. People did not prefer roaming or coming out after evening hour. I was also advised by the Hotel Manager not to go far after evening hour. But I was better in my room watching TV and sometimes watching people or vehicles on the road through the window glass. That was a phase when the entire Manipur was witnessing an anti-central government agitation led by some ethnic group. Screening of Hindi movies was not allowed in any theatre, neither were Hindi songs allowed to be sung by anybody or played by any audio devices. I could see a group of army personnel patrolling on the road very often bearing heavy arms. At the dead of the night too, I used to hear the sound of their angry metalled-sole dominate the road.

The next morning, I reached our office and found myself among unknown faces with affable eyes, as I was very young. People from every corner of India were there. I was greeted by one and all just like their family member. All day I stepped in each compartment of the office. It was a huge area with beautiful gardens, green trees, ponds, a playground, a residential area and a hospital. Tall eucalyptus and pine trees were all around along the boundary fencing and beyond that area, on the far outskirt of the city, the allurement of a chain of small hillocks covered with green forests that stole all your attention. The road, after touching our office gate, went distant after wandering aimlessly touching many other clachans, or green agricultural land, to get merged with the forest on those hillocks.

In the afternoon, I was told that the head of the office there wanted me to go to him. I was led by the peon to his chamber on the first floor among some scared eyes enough to scare me. But I knew he would be the first boss in my life, so I was very eager to meet him. I really had no idea of a boss in practical life. I stepped in and wished him. My boss looked like my favourite actor Danny Dangzoppa with a short haircut. He greeted me with a broad smile and a warm handshake. I was so impressed on seeing him, seeing the interior of his room that for me it took a few seconds to realise that he was greeting me with genuine warmth. He was tall and slim. He was in black goggles and a black suit just like a western movie-hero. He talked to me for long. He briefed me about my work, about the political situation of Manipur and all relevant aspects important to work safely in the field with the local people. That gentleman was a Mizo, as he briefed me about himself and about various communities and clans in Manipur. So, the man in me, who got to enter that room a few minutes ago bit scared, came out with a different and fair perception. I started sailing through all the waves from then onwards there in that office.

Then onwards I got myself shifted from that hotel to our officers' mess at Lamphel. I shifted from near "Asha-Jina" theatre or 'BOC' to 'Lamphel', near Regional Medical College (RMC), Imphal. Our mess-premise was very nice and spacious. There was a small playground and a huge garden for flowers and vegetables. Our mess in-charge, a local employee, was very caring. At that very duration, though I was the only person staying there, he used to ensure all comfort for me. I used to leave the mess exactly at 0900 am for office and return at around 0700 pm. I continued watching several movies in the theatres around on holidays.

Among the office staff, the ladies were seemingly in the majority. It was nice to see that women there had a very respectable stratum. They were as important and as free as men in every field of life. During rush hour, the streets remained crowded with office going women on their cycle, motorcycle or four-wheelers. In our office, most of the women used to come on their two-wheeler in groups. After parking the motorcycle under the parking-shade near the gate, they used to rush towards their respective work desk smiling and talking. All were found to be masters in their respective spheres. Women were treated with great respect in society there and they also used to enjoy equal liberty. They earned such respect by dint of their hard work and dedication for their family as well as for their society.

The famous 'Imma market' or 'Imma Keithel' of Imphal was worth seeing. It was being run by women. Shops were being run by women. Ladies, young or elderly, were doing all the work from bringing vegetables or crops to selling those to customers at the market.

During the lunch break, almost all of us used to come out to the teashop opposite the main gate for tea and take part in gossiping. We got all local snacks, fried vegetables or biscuits there. That small stall used to be jam packed and full of lively noise of men and women taking part in cracking jokes or arguments on political, social or national issues. That was a nice gathering. I knew all used to wait eagerly for those very few minutes in the noon to be free from all stress.

4.   Holy Thabal-Chongba

After a few days, the "Holi-festival" or "Dol-Yatra" -the festival of colours - pervaded all walks of life there. It is Holy "Thabal-chongba" in Manipuri. As per traditional practice, during that merry-making festival, which is to be continued for five or more days, young boys and girls, without much restraint, can mix, talk or dance with each other. At other times, the society of Vishnupriya-Manipuri is not enthusiastic about the mixing of boys and girls freely in their tender age. It is also a popular practice there that bachelors prefer to elope with their beloved one on that occasion. It is a major festival there, so its fascination lasts long.

One day I was on a local rickshaw on the way towards my office at Lamphelpat. After reaching the other side of Regional Medical College campus, I found a group of youngsters coming from the opposite direction, dancing and singing, showering or throwing coloured powder in the air. That vicinity was full of the cluster of huts and small houses, like a sub-urban area. The jolly group came near the rickshaw. The rickshaw driver was compelled to stop the rickshaw there. Boys and girls were dancing and playing one Manipuri song in the sound box. All of a sudden, from that group, a girl, in traditional Mekhla-Chaddar came to me. She was telling something which I could not follow due to the loud music. She was beautiful, her fair cheeks were puffed red and her unruly silky hairs were disturbing the painting of sandal paste on her forehead. She tried her best to convince me about something in Manipuri. In that huge noise all around I failed to understand what she was telling except some of the words sounded like "Paisa Peru". I was baffled to see her lose her temper as she all of a sudden jumped on the rickshaw, she was breathing abruptly with some mysterious sweet fragrance, and before I could guess anything more she swiftly took out my pen from my chest-pocket and ran away like a deer by jumping down from the rickshaw.

It took some moments for me to get back into sense and to realise about the loss. That golden-coloured fountain pen was invaluable for me for it was gifted by all my friends at my native place as their token of love at the railway station before I departed for Imphal. So I could not let that pen be snatched that way. I indeed jumped down from the rickshaw and opted to chase the girl like a leopard forgetting all about the time, place and everything. So it was a long chase on those narrow paths in between those houses, crossing some yards or garden. I was running behind the girl and that group of youngsters were behind me shouting heavily encouraging either the girl or me.

I started shouting, "Hey, you girl, give my pen back, please. Stop, see. Listen, what is wrong?"

I was sure that the girl was rather enjoying the race. She did not stop. But I ran much faster than her. So I crossed her and eventually blocked her way extending my hands on either side. She stopped. Then as I was dog tired, breathing heavily letting my body and arm to take rest on my waist and as I was not in a position to talk properly due to the want of breath, the girl started laughing. It was a hot day and I was sweating to the worst. The group behind me also reached there. Somehow, I convinced the group leader that I was very new there and also about the importance of that pen to me.

I found boys and girls discuss among themselves and I was lucky that one aged person from the neighbouring house intervened at that very moment and understood my problem, and the situation as well. He started rebuking them and told me about the traditional practice there to collect donation from people by such a group to celebrate the gala of Holi. The girl was actually asking for some donation from me in Manipuri. And as I failed to understand and respond accordingly, she got angry and snatched the pen. I regretted my foolish presumptions or assumptions.

The girl returned the pen with a smile and then I started smiling. I gave them a note of 50 rupees as my contribution for celebrating the festival of colour. They were immensely happy, and so was I. We wished each other good luck and Happy Holi. That day, I came to know that "Paisa peru" implied 'give money' and that "Nupi" was 'girl' or in the same way, "Mayang" meant 'non-local', 'outsiders' or mainlanders.

Pung Cholom: Soul of Classical Manipuri dance

However, for me it was thrilling to run behind those butter-white tender feet. Those were chase-worthy. I still love to remember that race to get back my pen. So I was gifted with some unforgettable touching moments in that

'Holi' in Imphal. I suppose I wasclose to falling deep into the fathomless sea of irresistible liking for that very different essence of sense in that very occasion. I still love to remember the way I was being smacked by the sweet fragrance of her sweaty forehead, the talcum powder, those trembling watery lips or the little white flowers on her long hair.

I was lucky to watch other festivals also with a very close view. One will be thrilled by seeing 'Thangta' dance, a martial-dance, by male dancers dancing with a sword in hand with extreme aptness and balance. Every step by those dancers on the background music by 'Khol' and 'Kartal' (or cymbals) in some unique tune was really striking and amazing. I was surprised to see the dancer remain in the air or to perform acrobatics, on the ground or in the air with 'khol', 'pung' or 'kartal' in their hand. It is very difficult to describe how the audience gets thrilled and attached with those dances of "Pung Cholom". I felt so proud witnessing the magnanimous extent or diversity of our culture. I was astonished at how people, since time immemorial, worked hard with honest devotion to let a sense of Indian art and culture or religious belief to get knitted together and to form such unique style to display what is in one's mind. I found people sobbing in joy for attaining the ecstasy of the nearness of God in a festival called 'Lai Haraoba' or any 'Kirtana'. Especially, the elders in the audiences watched such events with tearful eyes.

One day early in the morning, when I was on the way to the polo-ground for a morning walk, I came across some other groups, especially those of children, in procession with the photograph of Rabindranath Tagore and placards hailing Gurudev or Kabiguru as it was his birthday. Some girls in that group were leading a chorus singing 'jadi tor daak sooney keu na asey tobey ekla chalo rey...' in Bengali.

Very often, I used to attend our office at Mongsangei also. Mongsangei, a rural hub, was only a little while away from Imphal city. It was full of green paddy fields everywhere on either side of the black topped road. Canal-like water-ways was also running alongside the road. Villagers, both men and women, were found busy working in those paddy fields. Kids remained busy fishing in that canal with tiny nets. Tiny villages, congested with thatch huts, also with one or two RCC buildings, were also home to the huge greenery. And in that nice natural collage, there was a beautiful office complex of ours full of flower gardens. It was also famous for being the centre for various sports activities and good coaching. Hence the football ground, volleyball courts, boxing, taekwondo, badminton or kabadi courts were found crowded all over the day. So, it was lively watching players absolved in various athletic activities. It was in Mongsangei where I got the opportunity to witness the talent and capability of boys and girls of Manipur in all sorts of sports. They were physically so strong and flexible that it was quite unbelievable for me to not actually watch them on TV or cinema. Boys were warming up doing push ups with their hands, on their hands only, on the handstand position keeping their legs up in the air. I could not even dare to dream about myself to do that. I became envious of their fitness. It was Mongsangei where I saw people practising fencing. Those players used to fight, shrieking like real life heroes, and I imagined up historical figures in them. It was also wonderful seeing our boss there, a Sikh gentleman, always on his toe to ensure that no player was indulging any excuse to flee the course of practice and, at the same time, all office workers were doing their job in the office. I used to take part in the football matches in the evening very often, and then coming back to our mess at Imphal city exhausted, the wrapping of the cool breeze was soothing!

One morning when I was going to the office at Lamphelpat, I saw a huge crowd in front of the Regional Medical College. People were just rushing crazily towards the college compound. As I followed the crowd to reach the compound, somehow I could manage to peep at the centre of the crowd to have a look at the centre of all attention and became stunned by seeing dead bodies of five or six young men in police uniform. The previous evening those security personnel succumbed to bullet injuries following an ambush on their vehicle by some underground group just outside of Imphal city. Some seriously injured men were under treatment in that college. I found my legs shivering and my throat heavily dried, as it was the first time that I had seen sore dead bodies before my eyes and from such a short distance. All of them were local youths. Their relatives were wailing around the bodies. It was a shocking incident for me. What could those killers have achieved out of such an unpardonable crime? I was told, later on, that such killings are a tool to make terror prevail in the mind of the public.

Afterwards, I realised that as we got shocked and got our legs shivering the moment we saw the dead bodies, we actually helped those cruel men to achieve their goal, largely, as we might have spread the sense of fear also to others by being afraid. I came to know that such hard realities come more repeatedly. We will be witnessing helplessly more such helpless and hapless endings of tender lives actually caused for fulfilling the selfish goals of somebody else. End of all these may come after very long, only after we take heart to ignore all narrow domestic walls prevailing there around us, realising that those manmade walls exist only to exploit us. End of all such violence may become a reality only after we enable ourselves to make the state to visit our houses in the remotest of the remote, rendering true support to us to live with dignity. I could not find any reason that son of soils or fellow compatriots were being killed by their own people for achieving some fishy and selfish goal of a certain visionless people.

I discovered that like happiness sorrow needs no language to be expressed. Language is no bar there where people are shocked equally. When people are in grave shock it is either their eyes or face or even skin reveals what is there in their mind.

After a few days, I was asked to report at our office at Jiribum, a small town of Manipur adjacent to state-border with Assam near Shilchar. I felt relieved, as I will be at a fixed place to work independently. But some seniors in the office informed me that the area was volatile and one of the most disturbed zones in the Northeast. Almost all the ethnic extremist groups were active in that area fighting security forces or with other groups and so all those colleagues looked worried. But, I was not in the least tension or panic. So I was getting ready, showing no pout, to proceed to Jiribum and I started loving the name "Jiribum", as it sounded quite rhythmic to me. Actually my instinct always searched the good or probable good point in every new object or unknown place so that I could start liking or loving that place or object long before reaching that place or object. I was afraid that otherwise I might assess that place or object wrongly causing my staying there to be miserable or full of gloom.

But there seemed to be some other idea in the mind of the Almighty. Within two or three days, I got a new order or final order referring my place of posting as Kohima, Nagaland, though it did not make any difference to me. So I tried to forget all my presumptions about Jiribum. But I was happy that I got the opportunity to work at Kohima as I found Kohima to be a wonderful place while crossing during my bus-journey initially from Dimapur to Imphal. So I started preparing to proceed to Kohima after a few days.

5. Fascinating Kohima: Lost at First Sight

It was absolutely a sensation as if I was captured between a watery-cloud and heavy fog when we, the passengers, came out of the bus at the Kohima bus-terminus. I reached Kohima from Imphal. It was a welcome by a burst of fresh coldwater. Everything around was wet. Electric bulbs at the terminus and shops around were seemingly battling with fog and cloud to prove their luminous presence. Light and darkness were found playing hide and seek. It was cold and lively cold. Kohima at that moment remained veiled before me. I was in love with Kohima since I passed through the city a few days back and it was my second time to step in there.

Somehow, our office driver was able to trace me out. Hands in my wristwatch were indicating that it was exactly 9PM. All the passengers were in a hurry to reach their respective address or destination. To my utter surprise, I found most of the passengers who were to go to their own places on foot left their luggage unattended in the open at the terminus. As it was very difficult to get a private conveyance to carry their heavy luggage in that late hour and as it was very troublesome indeed to go up and down in the hilly track, with even a little weight in that drizzle, they supposed to come back in the morning to pick up their luggage. I was told that it was a normal practice here. It should be and must be the practice for everyone, everywhere. Unfortunately, there may be hardly any place known for witnessing such practice. Above all that practice was, or still is, in force there in Kohima not by any governmental, or by any organisational, dictate but it came straight from the sense of justice for their being "human", the greatest creation of the Almighty to pull forth humanity to go ahead and to lead the global civilisation to make this world a better place to co-exist. I was loving and admiring it. A huge tide of respect for the people of Nagaland pervaded my inner self. I was sure that in no place else it was advisable to leave one's belongings unguarded for a few seconds.

However, I started the journey for our Kohima office at Chedema, about 10 km away from the heart of the city. On the way to Chedema, I became spellbound on seeing that neither were the gates of any houses closed nor were two-wheelers such as cycle or motorcycles or four-wheelers kept inside the house. Those were found left in open and unguarded on the roadside. It was incredible that people there could not imagine that their belongings could be stolen or pilfered. I started loving such virtuous essences of Nagaland.

A glittering Zaphupeak, with a thin crown of ice on the top, greeted me the next bright morning. The dazzling sun in the clear blue sky and golden sunlight had made hills around so bright. The hilly terrain rich of forests and jhoom-kheti appeared to be dark-green sometimes and sometimes it turned silky-green. I thanked God from the core of my heart for preferring me to witness such a beautiful daybreak and to be part of such scenic beauty.

Our office complex was located along the slope of a hill. On the top of that hill, it was Chedema village and then down below it was a rivulet. In between the village and the rivulet was our campus. It was designed in such a way so that offices and all accommodations came up step by step along the slope of the hill, just beside the state highway towards Phek, the district headquarter of Phek District. The paddy field in the lap of the forest along the slope of the hill makes one love to keep on watching the collage of nature, seemed to be within touching distance but away from the busy life of Kohima. In the real sense, those slopping agricultural fields remained just living portraits in a different shade of green.

Then I met my colleagues in the office. It was a huge joint family of the Angamies, the Lothas, the Rengmas, the Aos, the Sangtams, the Chakesangs, the Semas, the Pochuries, the Koniyaks, the Zeilengs, the Dimosa-Kacharies, the Thankhuls, the Kukies, the Nepalies, the Manipuries, the Assameses, the Bengalies, the Biharies, the Arunachalies, the Odissies, the Telegus, the Tamils, the Keralians, the Kashmiries, the Rajasthanies, the Punjabies, the Marathis, the Garhwalies, the Santhals and many more. One could proudly say that was a huge joint family comprising people from every corner of India. The doctors, the engineers, the writers, the drivers, the sweepers, the barbers, the cobblers, the carpenters, the masons, the cooks and no master lived there to work in concert. All were doing their own duty and having a grand break with "fika chaa" (black tea) to get refreshed.

The sun set here by dropping itself silently behind the Zaphu peak after playing a bit with the black and white clouds. Hymns and bells from the churches were there to welcome the evening paving the way for the night. The chorus of villagers coming home from their field singing "hmm…. hmm…. hmm…aauuh…." and chirping of kinds of birds, who were seemingly desperately apprising their futile protest against the accession of the forthcoming darkness of night had made the moment of sundown more musical.

Very often, youths with a guitar in hand used to attribute the symphony. Nights seemed to pass quickly for us packed with sound sleep, and woke up to a cheery dawn added with hue and smile of villagers on their way to agricultural fields along the downward slope towards the foot of the hill, and the chirping birds busy discussing their days programme, was worthy to enable one to have a healthy start for the day ahead.

It was amazing to see the commitment and sacrifice of the women for the wellbeing of their family members, their home, their crops and every relevant thing. Most of the domestic work as well as the efforts put in farming were the contribution of the women folk. Even in government offices, women were found far ahead in performing or providing services for the entrusted task in comparison with that of the male folk. Rural women used to go to the field keeping food, water or even small kids or infants in the cane made a basket on their back. They used to work there day long to nurture the paddy or vegetables and to do their best to keep the field perfectly clean as for them that was their second home.

The most difficult part was their coming back home in the evening. Trekking upwards with a lot of weight on their back was really one of the toughest tasks. Coming up from the foothill to the village at the peak of the hill along a slippery and almost vertical foot-track was undoubtedly challenging. Every step needed extra support and caution. For those women reaching home exhausted did not bring on the end of a day's work or duty for them towards their family. Immediately after reaching home, they found themselves again busy in cleaning their house, preparing evening meal for family members, looking after the domestic pets such as dogs, pigs or poultry, offering foods to all and many other work before they finally go to sleep after praying to the Almighty for comfort and prosperity for all, except for themselves.

6. Bora Basti: My First Address in Nagaland

Initially one of my colleagues and I started residing on rent basis in the house of the chairman of "Bora Basti" near Don Bosco School. The humble house owner popularly known as "Baba" was always wearing a traditional loincloth and an impeccable smile.

Our house was a well-built construction with an ample lawn, parking zone, piece of cultivated land for Laipatta (green leaves of mustard), squash, rice, cabbage, cauliflower, beans, potatoes and numerous types of flowers. A small fishery, a small piggery and very small poultry, all surrounded by many quarries for collection of different varieties of flowers, green saplings or cactus which were also there in that compound. It was not less than a beautiful farmhouse. One who enjoys being reared near nature would definitely love to live in such a home. So, I was happy with my home away from home. Even remaining present in that house idly even in the holidays was refreshing.

Within a few days, I also started feeling proud considering myself one of the "Bora-Basti Manu," a man from "Bora Basti" (village), one of the largest villages of Asia. Residents there were also found very proud of their being part of that esteemed village. All the houses were picturesquely decorated with varieties of flowers, especially orchids.

People were religious, absolutely disciplined and committed. Sundays were heavenly with the gospel all around. Sundays were not merely holidays but holydays. I used to enjoy the Sundays doing nothing but witnessing the jovial mood and cheer all around there. Seeing girls with a flurry and lively hair, ever-running boys and benign elders returning from the church at the end the Morning Prayer was awesome. It used to make me realise that God was the eternal source of joy and He is omnipresent. Such an atmosphere used to make me feel submerged deep in the nearness of the supreme power and I could keep myself aloof from indulging in garnishing self-interest.

Most of my days at that house used to start by getting something the way kids use to get gifts from Santa Claus after their night dream. After opening our doors in the morning, I used to discover a heap of fresh Laipatta, ladies' fingers, beans or squash at the kitchen door, kept by "didi", daughter of the house owner. She had always been so caring. She used to instruct the house cleaners to keep our compound always dirt-free. Then there was a small pond full of various fishes, which was also a play zone for pet ducks. Hence, as a whole, it was a refreshing, healthy and safe staying. Playing football or badminton with kids was almost regular there. The sense of joy and easiness was found present in every corner of that vicinity.

It was also amazing to witness the agility and merriment of ever-running and ever-busy children of Don Bosco School. The roads and playground in the area remained full of cheer, tweeting and lively restlessness of the students while entering or leaving the school. There was a majestic presence of the school with its magnificent humming during the class hour, which used to blast out like an erupting volcano the moment the end-gong rang.

Then there were a number of other schools filled with boundless delight in that area. Kids with their tiny-little feet ruling the tough slopes of hills in the summer or in the rainy season or winter used to enthral me. As I used to follow the shortcut from Don Bosco School to B.S.F. gate at Chedema through the steep hilly foot-track, and I must admit initially I got my body knocked down once or twice on many occasions on those slopes, especially while going down. Soon I started mastering the act of falling down and, in the same way, I mastered climbing up along those slopes.

Going to the office by crossing the foot-tracks surrounded by vegetation, tiny paddy fields, farmhouses, bushes or forests happened to be very enchanting. On the way, I very often came across a small group of villagers rushing towards their "kheti", children running to their school, groups of boys or girls gossiping or practising singing under the tree. You were always greeted with a smile, "Bhaal achhey (How are you)?" or "Kot Jayachhey (Where are you going)?"Until I reached the B.S.F. gate, there were no crowds or noise. At the B.S.F. gate, the teashops or paan (beetle leaf) shops were the lifeline of the habitants of the surrounding villages a bit away from Kohima town. Sometimes while taking tea there, I was surprised seeing people's fixation there for devouring "Gutkha" or "Paan-Masala". Almost all the shops used to be decorated with strings of "Gutkha" pouches.

Walking down by following the Kohima-Phek road to reach our office was always pleasing. On our left, it was a hill covered with perennial greenery and narrow streams going down through the lap of boulders. The steep down-slope on the right side, providing a clear view of hills and greenery even up to Zakhama area was really worth seeing. The slope was extended up to far below down our heel, actually well-nourished cultivated land of villagers of Chedema and Borabasti of Kohima looked like a green valley within the forest. Those green cultivated lands going down step by step up to the river at the foothill were the work place for thousands of local farmers.

During the daytime, the cow shades in the middle of every single such farm used to remain crowded by family, including infants and kids playing joyfully in recess. Many times, serpentine white smoke continued coming out upwards from those cow shades as ladies cooked food there for all the members to make their day, full of hard work for good crops and a sort of outing for joy and picnic. Then in the evening, all of them used to climb up through the hilly steps with crops or vegetables on their back to reach their village, to their home. It was surprising to see how the village folks covered the distance from field to home every evening by climbing up and singing with a high breath and rhythm. Those ladies still kept some strength reserved to work at their home and to fulfil all demands of family members before surrendering themselves to deep sleep. It is possible only when one hates to allow any task to get better of him or her.

7. First Outing in the Field

The first field work entrusted to me was to conduct an integration camp along with our medical and veterinary wing in a village namely "Zilengrong" on Nagaland and Manipur border, behind Zaphu peak, far west of Kohima near Zaluki-Peren area. Our team was to reach the village late in the afternoon and to stay there for about seven days. So we started late in the morning. By the afternoon, we were just on the other side of the mighty "Zaphupeak" and it was amazing to find myself surrounded by deep greenery. Somewhere it was dark-green and in some patches it was a lighter shade. This part of Kohima was a few kilometres away from Zukhu valley, the green heaven of Nagaland. The floor of that beautiful hilly terrain at my feet was also green either due to long as well as short grasses or due to moss. The only other colour around was the black shade of the metal-road or a few red, white or violet coloured flower on the trees and clear blue sky above peeping through holes in roofs of green leaves. It was hard for me to believe that I was not far away from the urban life of Kohima. The valley full of several tiny lakes, wild streams and birds is worth witnessing, remembering and visiting again.

In many places, we asked the local villagers for the right direction. After some distance, the road was found very rugged, steep high and slippery. We then reached a junction which seemed to be a local market near our destination in the late evening. Though the shops or shades looked abandoned, about ten locals appeared from the darkness as our vehicle stopped. They came from behind the shops, behind the trees, in a moment. Something fishy was there in that darkness, in appearing of those people from that darkness and in the look of those villagers as I smelled. All those people were from Zilengrong village and they were council members of that village. They came to me and requested not to enter their village for some days as a huge group of Manipur based extremists was staying at that village that time for the transition of that entire group to enter Manipur in a phased manner from Zalukie area.

That underground group had made that village their rendezvous (R.V.) for the nonce. Hence the group was allowing none other than the villagers to enter into the area. I discovered tremendous fear and a sense of insecurity in the eyes of every member of our team. All the members, including Angami, Lotha, Chakesang, Sema, Thangkhul, Assamese and Nepali, were in the opinion that we would better leave that area before long. My conscience reacted wisely and conceded to leave that place. Those village heads rendered an honest apology for the inconvenience caused to us.

The same road that we crossed during daytime with joy, enjoying sightseeing and jolly chorus by the boys, appeared horrible making all of us speechless. Driver Chetry was courageous and apt enough to drive that tough road, mostly by using four wheels, saving us number of times from near inescapable skidding or those sorts of accidents. Nothing except the part of that road within the short range of headlight was visible. For some time we were not able to proceed forward due to dense fog. The heavy smoky fog was rushing towards us from all directions by storming the fog-light and headlight as if it would swallow us. The driver drove meticulously and after a fearful journey by following torn focus of those headlights for about two or three hours we got out of agony by seeing lights, though still far away from Kohima city and other hilltop villages. At about 10 pm, we somehow reached near Khonoma Village and some of the Angami boys proposed to contact the village heads so that we could halt there for the night and avoid any further journey at that late hour. We came down and approached the village council chairman for his help. The villagers were kind and courteous enough to welcome us and provide us with shelter and food that night. We were accommodated in the guest room of the church.

The way those villagers accepted us and rendered all help was not only laudable but also incomparable. The warmth seen in their eyes at that moment was so sincere, such that I had never ever seen in others other than my very near or dear ones. I was so obliged that my conscience bowed down before their true greatness. They understood the language of my eyes even though I was not vocal about my being grateful to them. I thought such an incident inspired one to stick to good and to do well in the true sense. We were gifted with such support and help at the time of actual need, and at the same time in that inauspicious night, for I or some of us might have done some good at some point of time.

The next day, early in the morning, the village council members and some youths came to us and we discussed our activities. I requested them to allow our team to carry out our training programme in that village. The village heads and youths had a discussion among them and then requested us to stay at their village and to carry out our programme. We happily agreed to our hosts and continued our camp there.

A small Naga village

Very often, when I go back to the past through memory lane I wrap myself up with those golden reminiscences. What I learnt from Nagaland and its people helped me a lot to acquire a better understanding of humanity. True education perhaps would have been merely, and largely, a farce without such lesson. From people there I have learnt to keep myself happy and content in any phase of life.

8. War Cemetery: Our Pride

I used to visit the war cemetery in Kohima regularly. It was the abode of great souls who left behind instances of extreme self-sacrifice for our country. The memory of those brave Indian soldiers was kept there as a burial in the disciplined pattern. That historical place, in the heart of Kohima town on Garrison Hill, really fill our heart with imagination about how those soldiers fought against the Japanese Army to keep this country safe and became immortal by sacrificing their life.

The monuments, graves, memory-stone, those epitaphs or inscriptions and all other things around make one nostalgic and make one convince as if he or she were one of those heroic Indian soldiers fighting that historic 'battle of Kohima' to defeat the will of aggressor to proceed any further into India as it was a must-win-war for us. Behind every tree or rock, one can find soldiers running and firing towards enemies coming in huge numbers from the 'tennis court' side. One can feel the wind coming by touching the quivering cheeks and clenching teeth of our soldiers who took an oath to fight till the end to ensure the safety of all of us. One can smell the scent of gunpowder or other combat accessories. He can terribly shiver by guessing the whistling sound by cartridges on the fray, piercing the air and almost touching one's lobes, forehead or hair. At some point of time, the whole arena used to turn into a "light & sound" show for ultra-sensitive minds. Then, after coming back to the reality one can discover himself among shrill or sweet chirping of birds or flowers or a colourful butterfly.

Then one can see the mute witness of the brave-struggle, the beautiful 'Cherry tree' near the tennis court. In fact, the present 'Cherry tree' is said to be the sprout from the original one which actually saw the war from within. It rendered cover to the soldiers. Like many other fighters, it received a lot of bullet injuries silently and laid its life there. The place is reminiscent of a great battle to keep the enemy away. The battle is also remembered as "Battle Under Cherry Tree". One lovely cherry tree, near the tennis court of that historic Garrison Hill sacrificed itself for being utilised as shield or cover to continue fire on the leading enemy troupes. Thankfully, that sapling or branch of cherry was nurtured in place of that very taciturn prey of that battle. The symbol of the cherry tree still compels us to be apprehensive. So within every tree or every stone or every hillock there has been a lot of facts to share with us, which they try to tell and sometimes they succeed to make us listen.

I loved to witness the all-round greenery in the periphery, the true freshness and variety of lots of flowers there. Tall and elderly trees all around, hosting varieties of birds, were soothing for the eyes and ears. The cemetery looked very neat and clean, but it was seemingly in need of more care, infrastructural support, projection, interest generating campaign or advertisement so that more people do turn up with family and kids to visit such a mesmerising place, one of very few of this kind in India. Children can have nearness to the real heroes.

I found the cemetery a place that let one be closer with the great souls who keep on inspiring us in every step of our life. All from the burial want us to do better for the country for which they laid their life selflessly. It seems not only a graveyard of about 2400 great Indian soldiers, not only some mere memory stones to retell the truth of the great war of Kohima in 1944 but also an inspiration for all sorts of struggles, and it will remain so for ever.

The great epitaph saying *"When you go home tell them of us and say for your tomorrow we gave our today"* has always been a great source of motivation for me. I honestly wish all those brave men to be born again in this country and to live long days in this independent India. They can tell us whether this nation is on the right track or otherwise. They deserve a lot more life. Very often, a musing overwhelms my innerself as to whether I or we really deserve those sacrifices or not? That holy place really inspires everyone to introspect sincerely. Who knows some of us were some of those soldiers or not? So, we should lead life to make those noble sacrifices worthy.

At least, some more care in maintaining sanctity and beauty of the place may display our honest respect and love for those great souls. Our silent submission with great esteem may make those brave souls be in real peace. Apart from those memory stones, the cemetery should have more details or information about every individual martyr, or digital devices to display the history of that great "Kohima-war", designed specially to attract schoolchildren. I have seen some kids offer flowers on those memory stones, in all most every memory-stone, by their little holy hands, with pure spontaneity, as a token of love and reverence for those unknown soldiers.

9. Guwahati to Dimapur, the Bay of the Northeast

I always preferred travelling by night-service buses between Guwahati and Dimapur while going home on leave. Those buses were comfortable, and moreover the road was incredibly smooth and soothing! Whether going towards Dimapur from Guwahati or in the opposite direction, I always used to wait eagerly to reach Jakhlabandha, one of my favourite bus-stops hosting many hotels, bars and numerous shops with varieties of consumable goods.

To me, that little place near Nogaon in Assam was a perfect place for night carnivals. I used to devour all activities there with my eyes. People rushed in to those hotels. Hoteliers used to shout to attract those passengers. Though every bus used to stop in front of a particular hotel where the bus staffs used to get food and drinks free of cost, the passengers used to disperse also to other hotels many times. All the paan-shops and shops for cassettes or CDs remained busy in competing with others by playing music in the highest pitch at a time. One could not guess what to listen. It was simply chaos, a jumble of "qawwali", western, "gazal", Hindi filmy-songs or "Bihu" music.

The bus staff would call for their respective passengers after their meal. I found more than 20 or 30 buses at the station there where as the same numbers of buses used to leave at a time from there to respective destinations. Some passengers, who were late, used to run behind the bus on the move. There seemed no point for anyone to be bored at Jakhlabandha. People from the whole of India would be seen gathered there at a time. I could wait there for hours doing nothing to witness the pulsation, the thundering wave of people of all races and all sects. But surprisingly I had never have had the opportunity to witness Jakhalabandha during day hour.

While coming from Guwahati for Kohima or Imphal by the night-super bus, one would be welcomed at Dimapur early in the morning. One could enjoy the warmth of the place by sipping hot tea and by having a glimpse of Nagaland, by going through the "Nagaland Post" or "Tribune", some of the beloved dailies of Northeast. That tea was good enough to get rid of drowsiness and tiredness. So it was really a refreshing break for the passengers who were to travel further towards Kohima or Imphal. One would get to Dimapur a bit cold in that early hour of the morning and one would feel the allurement by green hills all around.

In Dimapur, we had one transit house in a beautiful building just near Dimapur Airport. It was a big compound, full of flowers, fruits plantation and fisheries. The two-storied building in the middle was our accommodation and it was as good as a resort. I loved to stay at that house whenever I used to come to Dimapur. That transit house of ours was just on the approach road of the Airport going further to Ao-Imti village. Other surrounding villages, such as Padampukhuri, Naharbari, Darogapathar, Nagarjan or Burma-camp were also not very far. I visited those villages on various occasions.

The surrounding places, especially Chumukedima, Diphupar, Phaipajang or Patkai were really picturesque. Nature had assimilated all its beauty around those places. The hillock, rivers, stream, greeneries, dense forests, lots of flowers, fruits, farmland and everything else was there in plenty. Watching taking off and landing of the aircrafts on that runway in that deep green hilly background was really soothing for my eyes. It was a different world after crossing the Dimapur town, one of the busiest business hub of the Northeast.

In Dimapur, a cosmopolitan city, people from all over India were staying for their livelihood in peace. It was overwhelming to witness that people from all religion, all sects and all classes met and blended in that city and around since long.

It was claimed that the Pandava prince Bhima married to Dimasa Kachary princess Hidimba while the Pandavas were in exile. During the Mahabharata era, Dimapur and its surrounding places used to be the capital of Dimasa Kachary Empire. If the local tales are to be believed then Bhima's son Ghototkatch was born there. If one goes around out of Dimapur town he can find and feel that the river, stream, forest or hill there beckons some distinguished features. Even remains of the palace or other buildings of Dimasa Dynasty there compel one to love and think about those places. I liked roaming along the Dhansiripar river, the Dhansiri township and the nearby villages.

Once one of our drivers Sheli Ao met with a horrifying accident while driving the office ambassador car from Dimapur to Kohima. He was driving the car in high speed and as the car reached near Chumukedima, a village girl who was returning home after collecting firewood from a nearby sawmill with other village girls was hit with a huge blow. All of a sudden, that poor girl came in front of the car while crossing the road. Before the driver could react, the poor girl was struck. She succumbed then and there. The car was stopped after crashing with a roadside tree and the villagers out of rage drove Sheli for a long distance into the roadside cultivated land and then in the forest. But Sheli was fortunate as one Army vehicle patrolling party was crossing that area at that very moment for security checking, as on the very next day there was a visit programme of one VVIP, and appreciating the situation the Army took Sheli in there custody before the villagers could actually touch him. Villagers were demanding to hand over the driver to them, as they supposed he had no right to live any more. The army rescued the driver and handed him over to the local police.

Consequently, I was sent to Dimapur to talk to the parents and villagers so that the driver could be taken out of police custody. I went to jail and talked to Sheli, he was almost broken and he was found repenting. He stated that the girl had all of a sudden started running to cross the road leaving the group of her other friends on the other side of the road. And before he could do anything the girl was smashed to death. He also said that he was ready to admit any punishment for his mistake. He was mourning the death as he thought he could have controlled the vehicle, but he could not do so as the girl's movement gave him no chance. The Officer-in-charge of the police station advised that as the driver was on duty if the villagers could come to a negotiation and show mercy to the driver the case can be reviewed accordingly.

So, I dared to meet the village council chairman and other dignitaries to plead for mercy on behalf of the driver. The villagers were very angry and they wanted to kill Sheli, so they charged me vehemently. I was to face all their anger. Even then, I requested them to allow me to meet the parents of the girl. Following a long persuasion, I managed to convince the villagers as well as parents of the girl to allow me to meet them. The bereaved parents, the poor father and mother, only wept at that moment. Tears seemed to wash away the wreckage in our heart, to a great extent. By the grace of God, they talked to me at last. I tried to make them understand that their loss was irremediable and it was a permanent parting. But they could have mercy on Sheli a young man for the sake of peace of the soul of their beloved daughter. There was different tune or version also among some of the villagers who wanted the driver either to be in jail for good or to be hacked by the villagers. I was forced to leave the village on that occasion but I continued to try to convince the villagers afterwards by going there twice or thrice.

I visited the village again and again to convince those parents and the village authority for their mercy for Sheli. After 4-5 days, finally the love of the parents for their daughter won. They decided to forgive the driver. I thanked God and those parents. The village council rendered all help to me to get Sheli out of police custody. I went back to Kohima with Sheli. Later on, Sheli tried to give a good amount from his savings to the parents of that poor girl, but the generous parents declined to receive any such amounts.

10.   Second Rented Home

After a few months, I was shifted to another house as 'Bara baba' of Bara-Basti needed those rooms, where my colleague and I used to stay, as some of his children and grandchildren were coming to stay there. My new house was only a few minutes away from the old one. I got two good single bed-room-flats. Rooms were spacious. The new house owner, a middle aged widow, was residing alone in the adjacent flat. One of her daughters was married and her younger daughter Pammi was studying in Patkai College. Pammi was staying in the Patkai College hostel and used to come to home once in a month. She was free, frank and fond of music and friends. She loved to smile and I had never found her in need of reason or pretext for smiling.

Whenever Pammi remained at home for holidays a group of 5-6 of her friends used to come there in the evening. As all of friends were boys, her mother used to keep herself awake up to 10 o'clock or 11 o'clock in the night, which was considered to be very late. That group used to have fun, gossip, sing or sometimes used to listen Eric Clapton, Michel Jackson, Mick Jagger or Mithaniley keeping their sound system on its highest degree. I used to keep my door and window closed in all possible way to save my eardrum and to get asleep at the time. Her helpless mum used to apologise the next morning with her vocal eyes and silent mouth for the disturbance the previous night and I with my silent smile used to apprise her that I hardly had any problem.

Pammi was a driving force of joy. She was agile and tender like a butterfly, only a butterfly could not smile like her. In the morning, she was again jumping, running, singing or shrilling, watering or taking care of flowers, pots, helping her mother. Sometime she would chat with me hardly giving meany chance to open my mouth. "Uncle, you know what?" "You know this?" or "You know that?" Most of the time, she used to be in T-shirt and knee-long-jeans, a perfect match with her boy-cut hair and boyish nature. I started loving Eric Clapton's "Mamma, I am coming home…" or Mithaniley's "Kohimate thaka khan Michha laga phootani …" due to her.

She was also a good cook. She taught me how to boil "Laipatta", beans or cabbage by using 2-3 pulps of garlic and some pinch of salt. On Sundays, she sometimes volunteered to assist me in the kitchen by cleaning rice, cutting vegetables or by preparing tea.

Sometime she used to taunt me for my doing all work from sweeping to washing or cooking by myself like women would. She used to tease, "Uncle, your wife will be very lucky."

I used to respond, "But, I will do no such damn domestic work after marriage. I will not even wash my own hand before or after a meal, right."

She linked further after laughing, "Kiley apuni Naga-chookri na loi? (Why don't you marry a Naga girl?)"

"Hoi, hoi to, bhaal maiki pailey eku digdar nai! (Yes, I don't have any problem if I get a suitable one!)", I replied.

She then enquired, "What about your mother, will she accept her?"

"No, I will not take her at home. In case of my transfer from here I will make her stay at Dimapur." I used to make her angry. She pretended to be furious in anger and gave me a real punch on my bicep. We laughed loudly for long.

One Sunday after coming from church she came in my kitchen while I was cleaning rice sitting on a cane-stool at the door of the kitchen. Pammi came from behind and held my shoulder tight by allowing all her body weight on my back and said, "Hi, cleaning rice?"

I was already in an embarrassing situation because I started justifying in my mind that she was doing nothing wrong. However, I got a reply at once and said, "No, madam I was hypnotising all these rice so that they get changed into 'bhaat' but as a witch is disturbing my concentration now I will have to have the mercy of the pressure cooker."

She laughed in anger but did not allow my shoulder to be released from her clutch of arms and kept on with clueless nattering. At last, she asked, "Apuni Laipatta bhaal pai hola? (You like Laipatta. Don't you?)"

I said, "Yes, I love Laipatta."

She left my shoulder and rushed to their room by taking one of my steel-bowl. I was so relieved. But, within a few seconds she was back with that bowl packed with boiled Laipatta.

She again asked, "Malik, goru mangso khay na nakhay? (Malik, do you take beef?)"

"No, no, no" was my reply which sounded quite filmy.

She said smiling, "Aji ami Laipatta banaise de goru mangso halikina. Beshi … meetha! Today I have prepared beef with Laipatta. It tastes awesome. I know you don't take beef so I have taken out all beef-pieces from this bowl. See it is only Laipatta for you."

She offered me the bowl full of boiled Laipatta.

I lost myself in the bottom of a deep dark sea full of large octopuses staring at me with fire in their eyes. Somehow, I told her to keep that bowl on the side of the table. I started sweating.

She kept on giving various lectures on various issues. However, I was not actually listening to any of her important views or valuable suggestions. My terrified mind was storming around that bowl. I started blaming myself for declaring my being fond of Laipatta. I was sweating profusely. I visited all the ideas in my innerself in search of some way to get rid of that bowl full of Laipatta. Because I could not hurt her, neither I could let my sense of reservation to remain in limbo for taking or not taking certain kind of meat. By the grace of God, I found some escape route. All of a sudden, I tried to remember that I had some urgent work in my office, although it was Sunday. I made her believe that my office people were waiting for me since morning in the office and I was foolishly busy with preparing my meal forgetting that all my colleagues were attending the office. I told her that I will enjoy 'bhaat' with her 'Laipatta' just after coming back from office after an hour or so. She realised my urgency and felt so sorry that I would have to rush to my office on Sunday as well.

I got out of my house and roamed blank and block-headed here and there in Kohima town, witnessed the Sundays grace in the face of people in the road, in the local stadium, in the church. All were enjoying the joy of Sunday not realising the dilemma, the agony, the fear I was suffering from. Finally, I prayed to all form of Gods to forgive me as I was going to deceive the poor girl by saying that I enjoyed her dish.

I returned to my room after about two hours and found the house silent and realised that Pammi was not in the house. I did the wildest thing. I silently entered in my kitchen and got that bowl wrapped in newspaper and came out of my house like a thief with that bowl in my hand and walked for a while towards Don Bosco and as I found no body nearby to watch me I threw the bowl into a roadside bush. I kept on praying for mercy to God and to Pammi in my mind for doing that for my being compelled to be so weak. But she was so happy hearing from me that her dish was very relishing. I sincerely confessed to God that very night for my not being honest to Pammi. However, I only knew how difficult it was for me, to talk with her looking straight at her eyes.

11.   An Evening With Rice Beer at Kizoma

O ne day, we reached Kizoma village. Villagers were already contacted for our camp there and as we entered there, they extended a warm welcome. We reached that beautiful village after crossing Chakabama valley, hosting Army, as well as GREF, headquarters, on the gentle sloppy land. The village itself was on a valley type land, rich with flora and farmland. It had a huge church, school-building, community hall, health centre, good roads and as a whole it looked like a self-sufficient village. In the evening, after returning from their farm, or forest, people started gathering to meet us. The village council chairman came there and talked to us. He enquired whether we were comfortable in the room of the community hall or not. He ensured every aspects or arrangement for comfortable staying of our team there for some days.

We were invited by the chairman for dinner that day. His was a huge Naga-hut made of wood and bamboos. Huge wooden-logs fitted in triangular-shape on three large wooden beams, allowing a terrace or veranda under the same thatched-roof, was the front of that house with a clean yard. Bamboos or canes were nicely set on those woods to decorate the house uniquely. It was a huge family. The number of pets was also large, pigs and dogs were found comfortable to seat and roam with us. The large-horned-skull of 'Mithun' hanged beside the main door was worth seeing. Those proud horns were just shining.

I was overwhelmed by the warmth of the elderly chairman and his family. We sat in the kitchen of the house. The room was full of wooden stool and chairs with a huge fireplace or furnace in the middle, which was seemingly never ever been without fire since its coming into being. Without any hesitation, the chairman, with two-three chains of large beads of different colours on his chest, started talking about his family, his farmhouse and many more things. He was so jolly and rich of sense of humour that he laughed and made us laugh in his every sentence, though he was not able to clear whole sentences as all started laughing before he could complete the sense. We continued talking about our work, about our country, about my native place, about Nagaland while taking tea and roasted corn.

Then there came foaming homemade rice beer in huge local cups made of bamboo. Chairman offered me a cup of rice beer, foaming with off-white bubble spreading the wild sweet and sour scent. But as I had some reservation about taking certain drinks or food I apologised and requested my host for one more cup of tea.

The chairman seemed to have one of the best minds under the sky, he considered me to have one more cup of tea in a huge cup made of bamboo. He also lauded that I was not taking any such drinks. But he tried to brief me all about the good sides of their home made rice beer or "Madhu" and also all about the bad-effects of foreign liquor in particular. He also told us that he hated the so-called liquor or alcohol and warned all not to take foreign liquor. But he claimed that he would be the champion in consuming his beloved "Madhu (rice beer)". However, the chairman stated that he was drinking "Madhu" on that occasion as he got a new friend in me and as we got together there as wished by Almighty God.

But he came forward with a unique idea. He requested me to kiss his rice beer cup to honour the occasion by holding his cup, full of rice beer, before me. He stated proudly that he will happily drink the whole of drink (Madhu) on my behalf. Without any second thought, I kissed the cup with great pleasure and saw the childish joy in the eyes of the chairman. The fermented fragrance of "Madhu" pervaded in me through my nose as the grace of God. He and perhaps God would be very happy as I kissed the rice beer cup, held by the chairman. All started clapping. We cheered and wished triumph against all evils. I felt extremely honoured by honouring his wish.

For me it was one of the best parties of my life in that kitchen-cum-drawing room of the house of the chairman, seating encompassing the burning firewood, actually the woven where ladies were preparing food for all of us. The chairman was able to manage to understand "Nagamese" language a little and he did understand no other language except Angami. Therefore, it was very important for us to understand each other's emotion, clue and pause. We both did well to touch all the passage of our conversation and both of us enjoyed a lot. For the rest we were being helped by some of our Angami boys to translate our statements from Nagamese to Angami-language or Angami to Nagamese. Afterwards the Pastor led us to pray to God before starting our dinner. I cherished my favourite Naga dishes adorned with boiled beans, boiled squash and eggs, daal, chatni of raja-mircha (local chilly) and chicken cooked using no oil, no spices.

In the morning, I walked through all most all walk of the Kizoma village. Most of the houses were made of wooden-plank in typical Naga fashion. All the houses were having enough space for flower or gardening, though every corner of the village was full of greenery, rich in orchid and various unknown flowers.

Such unconventional round in and around rural Nagaland helped me a lot to realise that the proximity to nature-mother actually rendered to pave the way to proximity to God. I discovered that only the gifts of nature are the actual boon to carry forward our daily doings in a healthy way and we should prefer those gifts to make our life away from unnecessary complexity on the way towards leading a simple, happy and austere life. Those rural people were extremely happy and content only by having ability and wisdom to afford care and love for their siblings, neighbours, guests and to afford time and sincere faith in God, praying for, only for, His blessing to remain able till the end to work hard and harder without caring for any ephemeral merriment.

12.   Sky Kissing Pfutsero

Pfutsero, the small town on the hilltop on the way to
Phek or Tuensang from Kohima was of exotic beauty. It
was the highest township of Nagaland. This sub-divisional
town of Phek District was so beautiful that I loved to stay
there. That neat and clean habitation used to make all the
passengers travelling on the Kohima-Phek-Tuensang road
compelled to roam cheerfully there for shopping or having
some snacks or food. It was famous for its charming nature.
Every corner of Pfutsero had the assemblage of colourful
flowers of different kinds, it was heaven for the orchids.
Even the shops were found dressed with orchids hanging
from the roof or ceiling. That town at the top of the hill,
seemingly touching the sky, with beautiful wooden houses
in the lap of green forest, rich of pine and eucalyptus tree,
would have been the favourite destination for the tourists
as it was the centre of various areas or villages, rich with
the hereditary Chakesang-culture, in the south-eastern
part of Phek District. Pfutsero was also rich with various
fruits such as peaches, bananas, oranges and various other
unknown species.

The moment buses stopped at the bus stand, all the passengers used to rush to all directions for shopping or marketing and for having snacks, tea or meals. The vegetable shops were full of varieties of local green vegetables. Squash, Laipatta, potatoes, cucumbers, green leaves, Naga-tomato, Naga-mirch (chilly), corn, brinjal, cabbage, ladies' fingers, beans, rice, cereal etc. were available in plenty and all were too fresh to attract the passersby. For non-vegetarians, there were kinds of meat or local fishes or insects available in some stalls. There were so many shops for cosmetic and other consumables. So, Pfutsero was always lively, busy and happy.

I loved to take food in one Gorkha Hotel as it used to provide delicious Nagadishes. That hotel was always found crowded. The cabin, where we used to seat, was a balcony almost hanging from the hilly terrace and from the window there, the green hills of Phek or Chizami range could only be seen whereas down below the deep black ravine used to keep on apprising its shivering presence.

I stayed at Pfutsero for several times on several occasions. In one such event for our campaign, we arranged a cultural programme involving local schools and clubs. It was an effort to mobilise civic-action, medical or veterinary treatment camps in the surrounding villages had cultural events on the theme of National integration.

On that very occasion we also enjoyed the cricket world cup on TV, up to late night, in the house of one local schoolteacher. All cricket-crazy people, especially youths, from neighbours used to gather in that house to enjoy

Bird's eye view of Pfutsero town

with tea, frequently even though I did not see anybody to play cricket, at any moment, in the surrounding. We all witnessed the cyclone named Sanath Jayasurya in that world cup who ultimately led Sri Lanka to take away the world cup home. Those youths also used to work with us the whole day to decorate the venue or in looking after kids to practice various cultural performances and sports.

For various works, for travelling from Kohima to Phek via Pfutsero was almost frequent. At Chakhabama Army check-post, most of the time, all passengers and their belongings used to be checked by the Army personnel as per practice. In between Chakhabama and Kiphire, we used to be questioned very often by a patrolling team of Army or Assam Rifles on the road. Once while coming from Kohima to Phek, our vehicle was stopped by one Assam Rifle foot-patrolling party. The commander, with three stars on each of his shoulders, came to me and requested me to give him a lift up to Pfutsero as he had some urgent work there at their headquarters. That officer was a Sema-gentleman and looked less than 40 years old. I hardly had any other option and I did not think twice and shared my seat on our one-tonne vehicle with him. He kept his carbine by hiding in the rucksack on his lap. And to my utter surprise he removed all his stars on his shoulders and hid those in that rucksack. Then he explained that it was just a safety precaution. As in the case of their being confronted by any wrong person or group of persons (extremists) on the way those glittering stars on his shoulders or the arms would invite some unnecessary and ominous curiosity.

In Nagaland, some people cherished the feeling of abhorrence towards officers of the Armed Forces, bearing stars with coloured stripes or ribbon on their shoulders, and non-commissioned officers or other personnel bearing one, two or three stripes or chevrons on their sleeves or arms, as during the Army operation, as part of anti-insurgency drive in around 1954-59, mostly those members of Army were believed to be in the front to lead those operations. Combat or guerrilla actions were at random by Army and Underground group against each other throughout Nagaland during that period. In some places, the village guard came forward to assist the Army. But people who directly or indirectly bore the brunt or witnessed some bitter experiences by being mishandled, perhaps, by force personnel those days nourished a sort of hatred emotion towards those very ranks and files of Army, as well as of all security forces, and that ill feeling not yet been stopped to be succeeded from generation to generation. Consequently, in most of the Naga villages people were found not able to afford to be friendly with officers or JCOs or NCOs of any uniformed force, but they were at ease with constables, who were generally not having any such star or ribbon. Hence, when not with troupe such security personnel were found not in ease in disclosing their rank.

However, it was amazing visiting villages, such as Chizami, Kikruma, Metsulami or Lekhumi around Pfutsero and listening village folks, especially by youths. In every village I had easy access and it nicely turned into some sort of cordial affinity that whenever people from these areas came to Phek town, the district headquarter of Phek, they used to visit our office. Our long persuasion made us able to be considered as a friend of those locals. We convinced youths, both male and female, and their parents for sending those youths to other parts of this country as part of "Youth Exchange Programme". Such a trip or "Study-tour" to other states organised for the boys and girls were found fruitful to make them have a clear visual of this country and its diversity. They used to help in generating interest or curiosity among native villagers, about knowing various parts and people of India, while sharing their experience with people of their village after they return. All of those youths form remote villages were found to cherish a sense of honest reverence and pride once they complete such tours.

13. Phek, the Chakesang-Home

I had the privilege to stay for long days in various corner of Phek District. I visited almost every corner of that Chakesang-tribe dominated area from Chozuba to Phor. Chakesang language sounds nearer to the ascent of Angami. I stayed for long on the outskirts of Phek village. People of that village were proud of Chakesang-cultural-affinity, affable villagers and crops. The village itself was the Brigade headquarters of Naga-Army. Till that time, the area was declared as a "dry-area", i.e. nobody was allowed to consume foreign liquor. Hence, social discipline or ethic seemed to have utmost importance there in daily life.

I used to get up early in the morning in full of a tweet of various birds and smile or gossip by the village folks going to their kheti all around our office and accommodation, which was actually a very old bungalow reportedly used by the British. Some of the locals used to say it was a haunted house though we had never experienced any British ghost to roam or to make any fishy discussion or likeliness of occurring of ghostly anger so that we did not dare to stay there. I actually was very eager to meet some of such Ghosts. Initially, I used to sleep after waiting for long expecting some mysterious sound or sound of shadow changing into the carcass. Fortunately, nothing happened and I remained deprived.

Ladies from Phek village used to come in the morning to our campus with vegetables in the basket on their back. We used to buy potatoes, cabbage, beans, squash, green chilly or types of green leaves. All those vegetables were fresh from those farms up or down the hill. Local vegetables were really sweet and delicious because villagers used no chemical or artificial manure in the soil for agriculture. Those local products had been so appetising that one needed no extra spices or oil for any item or dish. However, those ladies used to change our campus full of colloquial by their breathless chattiness and laughing. Sometimes local boys used to come with fresh fishes from the hilly stream. Those were costly but tasted brilliant.

Three or four streams were bringing fresh and clean water, for villagers and us, from an unknown place at the top of the forest-covered hill. Those were perennial though the flow of water remained very less during summer. On Sunday, there used to be a huge crowd of ladies in particular for washing clothes at the stream near the Phek-Lossami road junction. They used to bring a heap of laundry in the basket on their back and those stream sites used to become picnic spots. Kids used to play either war-games or other nameless games, girls used to gossip or laugh in an unruly manner. Kids also enjoyed food by collecting firewood or dry grasses or leaves near the stream. Then they used to distribute those foods among themselves by their tiny soft hands and it was a real joy and a grand picnic.

Our office-accommodation and view of Phek village

On various occasions, I used to take a bath in the rivulet a bit away in the forest on Phek-Lossami road and it was like dating with nature. The way cold water thrilled the body on its first thrust, and then it used to pour such a sense of adoration in the whole of my physical being and soul, that it used to be very difficult to stop taking a bath or to come out from under the stream.

Sometimes, I tried to wash my heels by rubbing stream stone or boulder in local style and it worked wonderfully making me start believing that there was no dearth of natural soap or cosmetic here under the sky. I found villagers making salt by burning a banana tree. The latex of banana tree can give us the healthiest salt if burnt properly and it was claimed to be very good for the heart. In some villages, I enjoyed tea made of various leaves of local wild herbs with medicinal value. I witnessed people adopt local ritual or treatment for petty physical problems. I guessed they were able to have faith in all those so-called traditional treatments as they could read the symptom accurately. There was hardly any case of a problem with heart or blood pressure even among the elders because of healthy food habit.

The villages around Phek such as Phek-Basa, Lozaphuhu, Losami or Pholami were rich of bamboo bushes, hence use of bamboo or cane for making household goods, rooms, stool, hunting tools, traditional head gear or even mats were in abundant. Most of the precious green trees in the surroundings of Phek, some of which were the mute witnesses of the history of the area for centuries, were no more surviving because of the ongoing popular greed of making money by cutting trees. Types of wild deer, fox, beer or leopard or other nocturnal animals were common in the forest, especially during night hours. Very often, the silence of the night used to be breached by the typical call from a 'barking deer' or group of jackals. Those howls sounded shivering ethereal in the dead of the night when echoed from all the hills, all around, when I sometimes had some struggle with sleep.

The approach road of every village or even state highway remained horrible during rainy seasons or even in case of minor rain most of the roads in rural areas used to be in a miserable state. On a few kaccha roads, I experienced our driver lose control over the vehicle as the slippery road used to push the vehicle whimsically towards the canyon with unpredictable skidding of wheels on mud. On many occasions, I found our vehicle to stop after a long skidding exactly less than a few inches distance from falling down to deep black ravine ahead and I knew only God saved us to escape from any fatal consequence.

However, I saw neighbouring villagers rush in-group for rescue in case of any vehicle found trapped in any bad road. Regular community work helped to keep public places like church, school, community hall or playground be in a better shape. The practice of community work also helped to develop a sense of unity and fellow feeling. People were very proud of their native soil. Everything of their own village was of special significance to them. The dedication of people in any task, for or in the name of the community or social work was exemplary. People's participation for the community work on our appeal, for example, for repairing or preparing of village approach road or playground or steps or any sort of developmental work was spontaneous and outstanding and very often it used to take the shape of celebration or festival as villagers used to organise community lunches. All used to work to contribute to the society selflessly.

In Pholami village, I met an old man in his nineties, as agile as a 40 year old man, who briefed me about the glorious past of the Nagas, their war against intruders, war with enemy or rival whoever came to plunder their village, their strength and many other facts. He stated how he fought like a warrior against intruders, how he used to run to climb up or go down carrying wounded or an ill fellow warrior on his shoulder in the time of necessities. He was as cheerful as a kid to show his biceps or calf muscle. It was strange for me to see a man in his nineties flexing his muscles to become as strong as iron. He even shared his experience about how he used to enjoy throwing the head of his enemy apart in the course of war and he laughed showing all his bright and healthy teeth while expressing how he found human flesh to be the tastiest. I was struck initially, though afterwards he played 'panja' with me revealing his juvenile inner self. I took all care to win over that grand old man by losing to him.

In some villages, I met some people, though very less in number, who were still following worshipping nature such as the sun, the mountain, stone or tree, in their aboriginal way. They offered a lamp in the evening under some specific tree or boulder. It was amazing to see the feeble but sincere effort to get the primitive ritual or faith to survive silently and to continue a near isolated life, in some corner to do and to hope for the better for the community, the native land or the humanity as a whole.

Ever-smiling elder of Pholami village

14.   Lynie, the Tiny Valley: Climbing Phek Hill

'Lynie' a tiny hamlet on the Lynie river and at the road junction, where the road to Phek town took its own way for parting from the state highway towards Tuensang. It was truly a beautiful place. It was a very small valley, surrounded by high hills. The rocky hill of Ukhrul district of Manipur and the forest-covered hill of Phek of Nagaland looked like almost hanging on that spectacular piece of land. The nicely maintained cultivated land on the evenly curved slope was the main feature of Lynie. Different seasons used to adorn those cultivated land with different colours, during the rainy season those were deep green for the tender paddy or corn leaves and in winter or spring, it looked golden yellow prior to harvesting. It looked its best during autumn when those pieces of fields glowed with different green in different grids coming down step by step along the slope from high on the hill up to down where the river water running crazy on its rocky bed. The tiny magic land was also rich in kind of fruits such as banana, mango, peach, jackfruits or guava. That wild river was also full of varieties of fishes.

In Ukhrul or Manipur side of the river there was one Assam Rifle post on a small piece of small land beside the road. It was apparent that the place, surrounded by high hills, a wrong one to be a post of armed force. Such a post in such a place could survive only by depending on the mercy of the rivals. However, Lynie was popular among the truck drivers for its night stay, being in proximity to the Assam Rifle post, as they used to get food and lodging there in a few roadside inns.

Fortunately, I had the opportunity to stay at Lynie at nights, more than once, in roadside inn due to the dearth of vehicles towards Phek from Lynie. The villagers of the villages at the hilltop used to do most of their cultivation work at Lynie. It was amazing to watch villagers to climb up on their strong feet up to that unbelievable vertical height with a huge load and to go out of sight or to merge slowly with the forest on the top of the hill. Watching those great people going up and up singing Chakesang-songs until they vanished in their village was inspiring. I wished if I could do that.

Soon, in one auspicious night while halting at Lynie, I decided to pass the test by winning the ordeal by climbing to the top of the Phek hill. As it was surrounded by steep hills nights sounded very windy with a mild song of water of the Lynie river, running fast by smacking stones and rocks wildly on the way. The night, found to be motivating for me, ended with natural alarm by roosters on the roof and sweet or sweeter song and chirping of types of birds. It was one of the rarest occasions that I was waiting eagerly for the daybreak. Reddish sun light of the tender sun just reached the ridge of the hill, in Ukhrul area, on the other side of the river. Every corner of the valley was looking coppery red. Life in Lynie was just getting ready for venturing the day. Here and there, some trucks were groaning to get started after nightlong rest there. Drivers and helpers were busy checking their vehicles from every side. A few teashops were having some sippers waiting for hot tea before starting their journey. Some locals were in the river with small nets in search of fishes. Local elders were around the fire in groups enjoying hot tea.

I set off for reaching the top of the Phek hill by climbing the height on foot, by keeping a bottle full of water from the Lynie river and a packet of biscuits in my rucksack and of course I was full of confidence and zeal to reach the top. My enthusiasm overshadowed my nervousness. I started that adventurous journey or rock-climbing forwarding drastic steps. After walking a short distance on the Phek road from the junction, I followed the foot-track, generally used by the villagers as a short cut through bushes or the forest upwards. Those foot-tracks were steep and looked tough. I took heart, allowed a deep-breath, and started climbing following visible footprints of the villagers. Gradually, when I watched downwards through the gap of tree-branches, or leaves, and found the huts or shops at Lynie junction getting small and smaller. After climbing for almost half an hour, I found those footprints disappeared in a grassy slope or otherwise I might have missed following those footprints properly. Initially I got nervous and depressed as I was not able to see upwards properly for my sight was blocked by trees or steep rocks, and down below, it was a vertical ravine where one could see only blackish and grey clouds rushing down to get merged with deep black at the bottom of a seemingly fathomless gorge. A miss-step may result in one to get lost forever from everybody or everything in the world. A little carelessness could have caused me to get a bone-crashing fall from one rock to another.

Following footprints instead was found to be very easy. So I found myself almost lost on that forest on the steep slope of that hill. I knew going this side or that side might make my going astray more troublesome at that moment. However, mentally I was at the state of not looking back and I knew that there must be an end to the darkness or agony at some point on the path.

I decided to try to climb vertically straightway. I held the reachable tufts of grass tight in my fist and pushed my body upwards slowly with the help of my feet and knees by keeping my chest closer to the ground, like a reptile.

Slow and steady, I crossed the grassy slope and reached the Phek-Lynie road and found myself so relieved that I was safe and not lost in that forest-patch. After that, fatigue had never been able to get better of my joy of conquering every inch upwards of the steep Phek hill by my every single step. I enabled myself to gain the confidence "Yes, I can" and then after I crossed the Phek road several times but I was not allured to adopt a long safe route rather I followed a challenging steep track. Thus, after about three hours' severe ordeal I reached the southern side of Phek village the place I was well acquainted with. Then the real hero in me carried the tired body of mine to our campus. I felt immensely content.

Exotic Lynie valley

I, of course, missed my steps or slipped downwards more than once but at that moment, those were too trivial. An exhausted me took some own time relaxing by sitting in my room on my Jacket-shirt-trouser, all wet by sweating even in that winter, enjoying the dance of the jovial mind in a real tired body.

It would definitely be an easy game for a trained mountaineer but it was the most memorable achievement for me. I was happy up to the sky or beyond the sky as I discovered a winner in me. I was confident that I could climb all other hills steeper than that. Wiser only can win the joust. One surely wins when wisdom inspires. For me reaching Phek village by climbing such high was so satisfying. I felt blessed. So I was gifted with sleep as good as stupor like a mountain that night.

That day onwards, I started loving trekking one peak to another, village to village. I visited Pholami, Losami, Phek-Basa, Lozaphuhu and many other villages many a time from Phek on foot. I set off for trekking for distant villages so many times from Kiphire or Meluri later on and never ever, I got myself chocking out of fatigue.

15.

Amazing Meluri and Pochury People

:::

Very often I used to go to Meluri, which was another sub-division headquarters under Phek District. The Pochury-tribe dominated township looked like it was located on the hunch as its eastern part was on a dwarf hillock and came down with even and gentle sloppy terrain towards the west. This small town was worth seeing for its well-maintained houses, mostly made of wooden planks, around the local ground and in either side of the road. I liked this town for its lovely small market. Villagers from far away villages gathered there with a lot of known and unknown vegetables, fruits, trout-fishes, cages, baskets or fishing nets made of bamboo, Pochury-shawls or traditional attire and many other local products.

There were so many Manipuri traders to sell various clothing-items or footgear and electronics items, mostly from Myanmar via Manipur. They generally used to come there from Jessami area under the bordering Ukhrul district of Manipur.

Jessami, the beautiful small town where people, especially passengers from Kohima, Phek or Tuensng area loved purchasing goods from its market, was full of attractive foreign products, from blankets to slippers or electronics items, and of course this place was the hub of hotels where one would get Naga or Manipuri dishes.

The first time I visited Meluri was when one of our vehicles met with an accident, just in front of Meluri village, causing severe injury to a local young lady. The local police took the driver in their custody. I was at Phek at that time. The moment I came to know about the mishap, I rushed to Meluri and went straight to police station, and talked to the officer-in-charge there. He permitted me to meet our driver James Lotha.

I talked to James. He requested me to get him out by settling the matter after talking to the villagers. James was a young man in his early twenties and had just married. He stated that the road in that area in front of Meluri village was very narrow and that lady had suddenly come from the house compound in front of the truck and got struck before he could stop the vehicle. He somehow managed to stop the vehicle by braking at the right moment; otherwise it could have been deadly for the lady.

I met the village council chairman, an elderly person, to get his support so that I could meet the family of that injured lady. I was taken to the house of that lady. Her husband was very angry. In fact, he was furious and wanted to punish the driver. But he calmed down after a while and allowed me to talk. I apologised and tried to convince the man that it was not intentional on the part of the driver. I also met the lady. She got her right arm fractured and some big scratches on her two legs. It was a close save for her. She had gotten her right arm already plastered. She was blaming her ill fate as she had two kids and an elderly mother-in-law and father-in-law and she was unable to do any work at home as well as at their farm.

Her mother-in-law came with cups of tea for us and greeted me in 'Pochury' dialect with a broad smile, though I didn't know the language! But it did not matter as the smile led the conversation. I talked to all the family members. I tried to make them understood the agony of the poor driver, about his career. All of them tried to understand that the driver did not escape the spot after the accident but he volunteered to help that injured lady at that very moment. Everybody started appreciating James, and I was confident that they had forgiven the driver. I assured them that the driver would provide all support towards the expenditure for the treatment of that lady. I sought their mercy so that Lotha could be free from police custody.

So, the next morning we all went to the police station and requested the officer to help to get Lotha released. The officer-in-charge, a young man from Phek helped us a lot. I was surprised to see that none of those people displayed the least negative attitude. Finally, James was taken out of the police station. We came back to Phek with our vehicle. I got ample ambit to have some friends in Meluri following my association with locals after that accident. Afterwards, Lotha provided all support to that family as committed there.

However, I found Meluri as a centre of Pochury cultural affinity. The local church was the pivotal factor to get the locals to cherish all traditional Pochury cultural essence. Most of the time, the church compound used to be engaged well for hosting and grooming local cultural troupes besides religious practices. Local elders, boys and girls were always around the church for practising and performing gospel or other songs, traditional dances, etc.

Meluri was also the abode of football lovers. The local football ground remained busy throughout the year with football matches. People in general were crazy about football. Every afternoon there was a huge rush of players in the ground, as well as spectators around the ground for enjoying football. Some of the footballers possessed incredible fitness and skill. They could have been better players for sure if they had the scope to be trained under proper coaching. Skill and physical fitness seemed an inborn worth, as if gifted by God. Many a time, we witnessed matches between the various so-called famous teams from surrounding villages, or from even Phek or Jessami. Sometimes, marathon football competitions were starting from early in the morning and continuing up to late afternoon. On those days of marathon matches, Meluri used to host daylong fairs around the football ground.

I had many friends there in Meluri village and town. They were scattered in various parts of that round-shaped town. I loved to sit with them in their houses consuming cups of tea to chat for long. Drawing rooms of those wooden houses were absolutely neat and clean and everything was in the right place. One could easily guess that every small piece of casual thing was kept with the utmost care to decorate the room, as every house was considered there as the abode of God. The wooden-planked floor looked glazing astonishingly. One could hardly find such clean and shining utensils in the kitchen elsewhere. That actually reflected the love and dedication of people for wellbeing of their home and family.

Nonetheless, I would always like to remember my staying at Akhegow village. The hospitality shown by the villagers was overwhelming. Their warm welcome, and then accepting me as one of their close friends, earned a place in the core of my heart. I had the opportunity to stay at that village for 2-3 days. I visited every corner of that village; I stepped in their school, their church, their council office, their cultivating field. That Pochury village was like my own home. I did not miss any chance to visit that village on my way on Kiphire-Kohima road.

I very often got touched by knowing their valid hope and dream that their area will experience drastic development in the light of the Waziho-cement factory and Likimro hydro project. Every time I watched that cement factory, which was faraway but visible from Akhegow bus stand, I wished the factory would bring tangible development in that area too. The word 'development' is used here to perceive that the area as a whole was exclusively in need to have good road-communication, electricity, medical and education facility. It was already blessed with all rich natural wealth. I always appreciated those people living by knowing their limitation and to have small touchable dreams as those affordable dreams could make life worth living optimistically and happily.

16.   Watching Verdant to Weep

A s the state highway passing through Meluri town was the lifeline for the people of Kiphire, Wajeho, Phor, Akhego or Pungro area to remain connected with Kohima; Meluri town used to be the halting-station for vehicles plying to and from Kohima. Specially private trucks with a load of Fanta, a log of valuable teakwood, remained stationed there in huge numbers during the night.

There was a trend that most of the less educated youths getting inclined towards supplying huge quantity of log of teakwood or various other valuable trees, from the forests of Kiphire, Pungro, Moya or Wajiho area, in shape of railway slipper called "Fanta". People knew well that so-called "Fanta-economy", which was actually being run by various mafia or rackets having nationwide active network, was not only destroying forest resources and environment by forcing ill effect on the agro-based economy of the common villagers, but also destroying a whole generation of youths by alluring them to undermine their educational prospect or agricultural work and to remain adrift in search of easy money. But nobody offered any resistance. Hence, knowingly or unknowingly all were becoming part of conniving to make the land desiccated in the near future.

There was a huge flow of wagers, daily labours or coolie, from other states, especially from Bihar, who used to be sent to those far away forests for cutting and sizing of those century-old trees and then loading of the logs on trucks, bound for Dimapur. Those trucks with a maximum load of Fanta used to be on the run day and night to reach near Dimapur railway station. Sometimes those trucks used to sound "gno … gno … gno …" as if those were crying in tremendous pain.

There was no instance that "Fanta-economy" was able to bring any socio-economic development in any corner of Nagaland, except the fact that some mafias or gangs pocketed huge money. Their collaborators – spread over everywhere in administration, in police, in customs, in the forest department or even in some local body – got some money for keeping themselves deaf and dumb, for not raising their voice against the ongoing atrocities on forest valuables, in specific, and on natural assets of Nagaland, in general. Within a few days, I experienced how the bright green forest region of Kiphire, Waziho, Pungro or Sitimi area became pale and near barren. The green hill and hillock became bald. I felt so scared fearing that we might miss the green smile of Nagahills, we might miss birds, wild animals, flowers or even other bushes or grass in the near future; we might miss the water in rivulets or rivers, dew on morning grass or many other small but invaluable joys which kept Naga people to love their soil, their village so much. In the coming days such large scale deforestation will not only make Nagaland lose its most valuable assets but also cause all-round soil erosion which may result in us to lose cultivable land. I used to become very afraid of, and sometimes prey to, my emotion as well.

Verdant Naga hills losing its greenery

So wide was the network of their deforestation or 'Fanta-mafia' module that those racketeers were active inside Myanmar also. Hence all those invaluable trees in the vast forest spread over bordering zone of Nagaland, Manipur and Myanmar had become silent prey of greedy-irrational people, who did not mind to make the future of generations as well as the environmental balance of Nagaland and other states at stake for money.

No concrete or industrial development and nothing can be a sound substitute of forest or of even a single tree. However surrendering by the people silently before "Fanta-economy" was not at all agreeable. I could only pray that next morning onwards I will not find Fanta-rackets being allowed to have access to any forest. And I used to do that sincerely. I had a dream to see Nagaland grow up as a strong agro-based economy in the lap of forest and green-mountain.

Some of my local friends used to repent how Fanta-money was being concentrated in the pockets of powerful leaders or anti-socials or anti-nationals to make voice raised against the wrongdoing unheard! How Dimapur became Fanta-capital of Manipur-Nagaland region!

17. Kiphire: Home Away from Home

A fter a few months, I was sent to Kiphire to contact people there and to chalk out the spadework to establish our office there. Kiphire was a sub-divisional town of Tuensang district of Nagaland bordering with Myanmer in the east and in the south. Sangtam, Sema, Yimchuger and Tikhir were the main tribals dominating that sub-division.

In my initial days in Kiphire I used to stay in the P.W.D. Inspection Bungalow. The caretaker cum chowkidar, a Nepali, used to cook delicious dishes. In those days, there was only one Nagaland State Transport bus plying in between Kohima and Kiphire or Tuensang and that was also very irregular. Besides there was one private mini bus also running at times up to Dimapur via Kohima.

It was a tedious journey of almost 12 hours from Kohima to Kiphire and three or four more hours were needed for the journey in between Kiphire and Dimapur. Some hilly patches, consisting of a lot of U-turns to come repeatedly, after and before leaving and reaching Phutsero, Jessami, Meluri and Akhegwo appeared to be unending and taking a test of our patience. Even then, one could enjoy the journey in fair weather taking Naga meals at Phutsero and Jessami or tea and roasted corn or other snacks at Chakabama and Akhegwo or at many other places. But during the rainy season it was very difficult to reach one's destination smoothly as the road actually became a death-trap in some places due to heavy traffic of Fanta-trucks carrying huge loads.

In those days in Kiphire, the electricity supply was so irregular and weak that it was normal to experience load shedding for 18-20 hours a day. In the evening, the voltage remained so low that one could see filaments to choke in shame. None could read anything before that light. Then there was no telephone facility to talk with people from places other than Kiphire town as the telephone exchange there could only communicate with a local connection. The only means of communication for the public to contact people from beyond Kiphire was the postal service. So, for that very purpose we were in the mercy of the efficiency of the postal department. The Post Office employees were of great importance in the eyes of all. However, I believed that we used to believe in "no-news is as good as good-news". Concisely, it always gave a gloomy impression about Kiphire. I was also not any exception as what I was fed by other people about Kiphire was not at all encouraging.

But, I did prefer to see things by my own eyes and not by ears. I reached Kiphire in the evening when the light was fading out. I took shelter in the P.W.D. Inspection Bungalow and had to have a candle light dinner, alone in that big dining-room, though electricity supply was there at that moment. People were found walking on the road with torch light in their hand.

Next morning, I got up to find myself in bright sunlight. I came out and introduced myself with the air and essence of Kiphire. Trees, flowers, roads, houses, green hills were all looking bright. I did truly love the atmosphere very much. Most of the houses and shops were found made of wooden planks. Those nicely maintained houses, or even shops, on both side of the road were worth watching. Roads were clean, though not well-maintained. Most of the roadside houses were two-storied with the ground floor under the road level.

As I came at Kiphire to organise a campaign so that we could reach and convince people about our concern towards supporting the locals for their all-round development and to lead people to be concerned about the nation and nationalism. I started reaching people of all types. That was my first visit to Kiphire but people were found so friendly and courteous that I got everything at ease. Local dignitaries, some fatherly and some elder brotherly, heard me and promised to render all possible help to make the campaign successful. I worked hard to approach various local bodies such as churches, women associations, youth clubs and schools for inviting them to support me and to enrich the programme by taking part. Those affable locals made me stop feeling alone.

Within a few days, I realised that no matter how developed or rich in amenities a place may be but it is only the people of the place who matter whether you like the place or not! One can love a place, or connect himself with that place, if only if he finds friends there. It was simply discovering bonhomie and I found myself among bright people with wise minds. It was really a blessing to have support and guidance from all the local State Govt Officers. Most of them had been benign enough to consider me as one of them or as one of their family members. I was busy convincing people at all levels throughout the day to get our programme and perception accepted by all, and hence on various occasions I took my breakfast or lunch or elevenses with different families as if it were my native place.

The sole motto of our campaign there was to get ourselves closer to the locals and convince people how government machinery was honestly concerned towards the wellbeing of the deprived people of this far-flung border area. To know the perception of those people who despite all deprivation or adversity never displayed the propensity to leave their native place, which actually resulted in consolidating our will and strength to keep our border secured. To have a broader view of the local people about how the government could plan for the betterment of the border keeping sovereignty and interest of people of every clan or region intact by feeling the pulse of the mass. It was of the top most priority. I discussed with village committees of all surrounding villages such as Kiphire, Singrep, Phelongre, Amhator, Anatongre, Sanphure, Kesitong, Kiphire town committee and school authorities and decided to organise all programmes involving all the villagers, at the playground of Kiphire Government High

School. All the heads took the occasion as their own festival. I got a huge team of people from every class of Kiphire.

I was told by my headquarters that the DGP of Nagaland would be there as the chief guest. So, it was a huge responsibility for me to keep every presentation at the right place and time and to judge all pulses rightly, because at that very time there were some other realities in Kiphire. Two factions of NSCN were vigorously active there to prove superiority over each other and to continue dominating the area. Literally, two factions of NSCN and Assam Rifles were always hyperactive there to pose or play inimical among themselves. Stray firing or bloodshed among those three challengers in different parts of Kiphire was frequent in those days. At that time, keeping equal apathy and distance from those three vertexes of security triangle prevailing there was the safest way.

Our chief guest rejected the idea of coming to Kiphire on that occasion by a helicopter and he insisted on travelling all the way from Kohima to Kiphire by road. It was a wise and tough decision on the part of the DGP as it was his maiden visit to Kiphire area. As the area from Kohima to Meluri deemed to be posing no major security-threat for our guest but there were some hesitations in our hierarchy about his security pertaining to his road journey, particularly from Meluri up to Kiphire in the Tuensang district. Hence, we were to ascertain his road journey from Meluri to Kiphire to remain safe and smooth. I met various leaders in the Kiphire area who were key men to work as opinion builders for either NSCN (IM) or NSCN(K) directly or indirectly. I sought their help to get the consent of those underground groups to make the visit of the DGP out of any sort of uncertainty or any saboteur activity. My genuine appeal to those groups through my friends might have considered genuine acumen and immensity. So from my side I ensured our hierarchy that there would be no hostility, or untoward reaction or action to that visit in any part of the said area.

But the Assam Rifles authority was against organising such a programme, involving huge people including VIPs in an open venue, on security grounds. I again contacted each faction of NSCN through reliable people. I was able to ensure that no faction was against organising that programme in an open ground as the programme was found mobilising people of all squares in Kiphire and its surroundings. I convinced the Commanding Officer from Assam Rifles that no untoward outcome would be there in organising the campaign on the local ground. He insisted so that at least the opening ceremony involving VIPs could be organised within their campus. But that was not acceptable as by the time it took the shape of a mass-programme, we got all moral and physical support and encouragement from all sections of people to go ahead. I realised that there was a sense of healthy competition among schools, clubs or village cultural troupes to come forward with cultural performance. I was invited to watch their preparations, rehearsal and pace. Every participating organisation was on their toe for the final day.

The blunder took place exactly two days before the programme. Our senior officers reached there with the message directing the opening programme to be postponed for two days due to some important commitment by our chief guest. It was like a thunderbolt out of the blue for us, and for me in particular. Everything was finalised. Students sacrificed their study to a great extent, school authorities planned to coordinate and reconsider the school break because besides cultural programmes, sports events were also there. As the opening day's ceremony was the most important of the six days programme, all concentration of the participants was to how to make that day colourful and the performance gorgeous. Somehow, all participants and village bodies were conveyed about the sudden change in programme and the postponement of all activities for two days.

Kids especially took the news as very discouraging. It was very upsetting for one and all there, because managing the preparation for each item needed enormous persuasion, logistics and patience. The traditional dance by various villages actually involved a huge number of people and possessions. So it was a great disappointment for me as it extracted plenty of toil to make all to come forward in my support. I kept my teeth gritted and left everything up to the God and the wisdom of the locals, after conveying them about the change of dates, and had the outline for our out-of-Kiphire activity, including organising free medical and veterinary treatment camp in the surrounding and far-flung villages to remain flawless. As no telephone facility or speedy postal service was at hand there in those days, communicating any message to far away villages was a very tough deal. But all the villages were somehow conveyed accordingly by sending messengers from the Kiphire town. Those wise villagers also responded positively. Even then, those two nights were almost sleepless for me. The night prior to the opening programme was horrible because I did not know how cultural troupes from far away villages would be reacting.

At the very dawn of the D-day, i.e. the opening ceremony, I witnessed how the darkness and the silence of the dead of night gradually changed by being touched by the daylight as I had an almost sleepless night, seemingly as long as the longest. All of a sudden, in between the all-round chirruping, I heard some roar coming from far away hills. It was actually something I was eagerly waiting for, it was really something different. I got up from my bed like a spring and came out of my room. It was a chorus "auhh … ohho … auhh … ohho …" coming from the Singrep hill side. It was the sound of hope for me.

The sun just started peeping from the torn-cloud to show its red face making the Singrep hill and all clouds around it to glittering red. The sun appeared before me as a source of trust and strength to conquer all darkness and depression. I could see crowds coming down along the slope of the hill singing in a traditional rhythm on that tranquil and reddish background. It was the dance troupe of Singrep village coming down to perform that day. I saw a huge group of people in bright red, white and black coloured traditional attire. They were heading to the resident of the Commandant of Village Guard, who was a resident of Singrep village. They were to take rest there for a while before coming to the venue. The coming down of those villagers flushed a fresh air of hope and energy in all corner of Kiphire. I could hear children shouting in joy in different lanes.

I shook off all the despair and got myself ready to offer every good thing to have a chance. Those villagers took a lot of pain to reach Kiphire as per their commitment. I did salute their wisdom and thanked from the deepest part of my heart for helping me to get back my zeal. Within an hour or so, a dance troupe of Amhator and Phelongre reached there. Their roar and sound of spear striking the road, and sometimes on the shield, made everybody in Kiphire awake and rush to the venue. It was full of lively crowds to witness the colourful opening ceremony. Our chief guest, the DGP of Nagaland was stunned by witnessing the spontaneous participation of the local people in that programme, in Kiphire far away from Kohima or any of the other major cities of Nagaland.

18.

Sanphure Village: My Saviour

I visited Sanphure village on various occasions. Once I stayed for one week at a stretch at that village. It was about 20 kilometres away from Kiphire towards Kohima and also 2-3 kilometres from the Kohima-Kiphire state highway and on the road towards Sitimi, through the deep forest on the hilly terrain. A village-level camp was organised there by involving boys and girls from various other surrounding villages, such as Tetheho, Kiphire, Sitimi, Natsumi, Knoromi, Anatongre, Longmatra, Meluri and Akhegwo for better interaction through educational classes, and to make the youth aware more about the country, the state and the world as well. Classes consisting of geography, history, social studies, our constitution, first aid, etc. by our staff, as well as local school-teachers and village elders were found to be interest generating for them as well as common villagers. We used to have group discussions among them on various issues. During classes, we used to give emphasis to make them aware about our fundamental duties and rights, our constitution or freedom struggle. They used to take a keen interest and tried their best to understand.

One day, while I was explaining the significance of the various colours of our national flag, one youth came forward and described the same significance in his own version. He said, "Sir, ami bhabnatey amakhan national flagtey thaka 'saffron' colour aslitey 'daali', 'white' colour pora 'bhaat' aru 'green' to 'sabji' ke bujhaai di achhey de. Etu flag to asaltey amakhan life kei bujhai di achey de. [Sir, I think the 'saffron' in our national flag is actually defining 'dal' (soup of pea), that 'white' is actually rice and 'vegetables' are being represented by the 'green' colour. So the flag actually represents our life.]" He was serious.

All others joined him, "hoi to, ... hoi to, ... hochha achhey to (Yes... yes... He is very much right)."

I was spellbound. It sounded so great to me! I had never thought in that way. How nicely he linked our national flag with our life!

All of us used to go also to nearby farm-area in the morning to learn or to understand more about better agriculture or better irrigation. We played volleyball or football in the afternoon. In the evening, we used to have a cultural programme, in which boys and girls used to perform western, Hindi or Nagamese songs.

One of our staff Myangthango Lotha, one of the best guitarists I had ever met, used to sing"Lakho hain iha dilwale, aaoor (as he used to pronounce) pyar nahi karta..." and play the guitar. I was really lucky that I heard the Naga boy, hardly 19 years old sing such old Hindi songs with his fingers aptly going through all major or minor chords of the guitar in the evening in a remote village. It was simply awesome.

Sometimes, we along with the villagers used to carry out civic exertions, volunteering for community work. I was proud that one day we repaired the long village approach road, connecting the village with the state highway. All the males and females including the elders of Sanphure and Tetheyo village worked enthusiastically the whole day to mend all the potholes or eroded parts of the road. Genuine concern and innovation on the part of the villagers were found deserving all praise. They were masters in repairing the wooden culvert by using branches of pine trees. They were bringing heavy boulders from faraway for plinth work of the road. Land slide prone areas were also being mended carefully by using soil, pebble, wood or grass. They were working restlessly by singing Sangtam songs with a good chorus.

The Village Council Chairman Mr. Khamong and gaonburas also organised a nice community lunch that day at the church premises. The chairman was a good friend of mine. He was very active, young and honestly committed for the wellbeing of the village and villagers.

The village was on the top ridge of the hill; hence it was away from any water resources or natural stream. Even then, there was ample water supply from water reservoirs through the pipe. The primary school, the church and community halls were neat and clean. Roads in the village were clean and well-maintained.

Above all, those villagers were polite and friendly. I never felt like I was away from home and kin. I yielded very good influence among the youths of the village. They used to obey me in true spirit. All the villagers knew me and I knew all of them. Kids tried their best to teach me how to hunt fowls or crane. They took me to visit a stream in the nearby forest which was like a hot spring.

Coming down from Sanphure to the state highway after going a few kilometres towards Meluri was a tiny roadside village called Knoromi. The village was extended on either side of the state highway, but it was really deprived and backwards. I had good relations with the village heads. This village used to become transit route R.V.(rendezvous) or base for underground groups very often. The people of such villages unfortunately used to be squeezed by underground outfits, the armed forces, mafias and all. But they had never been considered for any favour for the wellbeing of the village from any end. Despite various such adversities, villagers were always found courteous and helpful. Once I halted at night at that village when our loaded truck had some defects in the engine during late in the night. The driver and I were provided with food and room to sleep in the late night. Afterwards, many a time we used to have tea in this village while going to Kohima. Some of the boys and girls were always found ready to take part in our camp organised even in other faraway villages.

In the beginning, I referred Sanphure village as my saviour. Well I will definitely come to that very fact at the right moment. Sometimes, life pushes you in debt in such a way that you remain in no position to repay that in kind throughout all your life. Best is the support that you receive unconsciously, where you even cannot guess who has rendered the helping hand in your need. Sometimes you realise that you cannot get through without help by others but you are not in a position to seek help from anybody for that matter and even then, somebody appears there to save you from imminent danger, be sure that God has planned that person to come for your rescue. Hence we should always try to help others as it is actually God who is helping the needy by using us. Moreover, we never know that at some point of time we may need help from one or more such person who you never expect to come to your help. That village was really a very, very important place, I should say, in my life.

19.   Visit Tikhir Hamlet

Anatongre village was in the far north of Kiphire town, just after Phelongre village busstop, towards Tuensang. That Tikhir tribe dominated village was just beside the state highway. So this village could be reached easily from Kiphire, subject to the availability of a vehicle. The village was located on the lower part of the slope of a high hill covered with deep forest. The east of the village was quite open and one could easily reach the high way by walking a few minutes.

Tikhirs were a great warrior and their dialect was nearer to that of the Sangtam language. Long back, these "Tukhialiu" tribes settled themselves in the basin between or around 'Zinky' river and 'Yayi' river near Kiphire of Tuensang district. As time passed, they were being referred to as 'Tikhir'. Sangtams used to pronounce them as 'Tikhiru' and in Sema dialect they referred to as 'Tukhami'. There were a number of Tikhir villages in Arunachal Pradesh as well as in neighbouring Myanmar.

It was told that in Kiphire region, these people first got settled at Anatongre village after appearing from a stone cave at Tongkhim area, bit away from Anatongre. So this village was of great importance in the history of the 'Tikhir' tribe. However, those people were still a bit backwards and less in number comparatively. Villagers were mostly poor. Most of the houses were thatched or made of bamboo and wood in the typical Naga style. But the cleanliness and beauty of the village cottages were worth witnessing. All the houses were nicely decorated with a garden and with plenty of flowers and green trees accommodating types of orchids. I met the village elders and did listen to their glorious fighting against intruders or about their head hunting. Some of those houses were still having a chain of human-skull displayed on the top of doors or the main entrance to enable all to recollect their past pride.

I talked to the youths, some of them had been in Kiphire for high schooling and one or two were in college in Kohima or Dimapur. They were in the dark about their future, whether to go for rural life doing agricultural work or to go for any other profession. I remained with them for the whole day.

I found that the area was rich in all potentials to become the hub of the agro-based economy. Less educated or illiterate people could choose agriculture, farming, poultry, rearing cattle or pisciculture, as their profession or for their livelihood after undergoing the necessary training. Natural vegetation or fertile soil of the area was certainly supportive for any agro-based work or industry there. The government should come up with sufficient training institutes or vocational schools to guide and support the youths so that they take a keen interest, with pride, in agriculture-oriented activities as their profession. With some infrastructural support, people in that region can ensure profound changes in the socio-economic scenario.

After a few days of my visiting Anatongre village one early morning there was a heavy knock on my door. It was around 0530 hours in the morning. I heard the mumble of a crowd out of my door. I opened the door and found the chairman and gaonburas of Anatongre village there and they looked very anxious. They sat in my room and narrated that previous night troupe of Assam Rifles, the sentinel of the Northeast, raided their village in search of NSCN(K) group.

The villagers stated that since some days a group of that underground outfit was camping there by choosing the forest area near their village as a temporary base. Assam Rifles raided the area and might have captured some of the rebels after an exchange of fire from both the sides. After that operation, Assam Rifles carried out random searching of every house in the village and in that course, they picked up one local boy under suspicion. Assam Rifles did not lend their ear to any request or reasoning of the villagers. Generally immediate after such raid or similar operation the male members of the nearest village, except kids and elders, used to run away to the forest for saving themselves from the atrocities usually carried out by police or force personnel in the name of questioning or interrogation. Any suspicion by the force personnel, not well acquainted with the local language, used to result in the male-member or members to be captured for further examination.

Villagers were afraid that the boy, namely Alem, might have been kept in the Assam Rifles camp along with the captured underground cadres. Villagers went to request the Commandant to let the boy go back to the village. At that time, they were coming back from the gate of 15th Assam Rifles as they were not allowed to enter and meet the Commanding officer. In fact, villagers were in Kiphire since 0400hrs in the morning. They knocked many other doors to get the boy released safely. And as a last resort they came to me. I went to the Commandant, who knew me well, and to whom I had easy access. We had a long discussion. I tried my best to convince him about the antecedent and activities of the boy, who was a student of Kiphire Govt. High School. I knew the boy personally, as he had done village-level training of ours. Assam Rifles had doubt that the boy was working with that group, directly or indirectly, and he was not actually resident of Anatongre village.

The Commandant took his time and, at last, he said, "Ok, Malik if you say so, we can release him. However, see, there are some formalities. Please, go through those."

He again said, "He will be allowed to go only for you. Take care that whatever stated about him by you is true and fact." He also briefed about their helplessness about such operation and compulsion in apprehending such youths, after such operation, for gathering more information about those groups and for ensuring better command over the area.

There were certain formalities. I was told to endorse in black and white that the subject was taken out of Assam

Rifles custody in good physical and mental state. I signed every paper and then they handed over a certificate to me, declaring the boy as "White".

I talked to the medical officer of Assam Rifles, who was a good friend of mine. He confessed that the boy had have faced some third degree treatment in the course of interrogation.

Then after, I was taken in front of the room where all the subjects were kept. The room was locked and heavily guarded. I entered the room along with the doctor. It was so dark inside that nothing was visible. But there was a smell of rotten dampness, I could vomit anytime, and I heard some sigh and groaning by a male voice. It was very shocking. I knew all the men in that room must be weeping or moaning out of pain as they faced vigorous tortures during interrogation.

I whispered, "Alem."

There was no response. Perhaps, Alem, the very boy, responded but the sound might not reach to me. I again called in bit louder voice, "Alem."

"Sir, here I am," Alem's near inaudible voice came from a far corner.

One Assam Rifle jawan went to that corner with a torch and brought Alem to me. We then left the room. It was really pathetic to see Alem, a 17 year old boy, in that condition. His facial-skin was nearly bruised by heavy boxing near cheek and eyebrow. He was beaten blue and black. His eyes were swelled to look like a black cricket ball and there was a blood clot. He could not open his eyes. His lips were smashed. Blackish red stripes were there on his palm and arms. He was not able to stand straight. There was heavy swelling on his feet and lower abdomen. He was beaten with stick throughout all his muscle of his legs and hands. He was not in a position to touch the ground by his left leg. His nails were also not spared.

I hold him tight. He extended his right hand across my soldier for support and that poor boy came out of the camp on his right leg. The village chairman was waiting bit away with one jeep. We came straight to our office.

When I asked Alem about what he was asked during interrogation. He answered that he was not asked a single question. He said that he was just thrashed, boxed, hit with a stick or kicked by those constabularies restlessly. He smiled with his smashed lips and said that since his childhood he used to cherish the dream to join the army. He said with a sad smile, "Bachcha thaka time pora ami Indian Army te jaboley beshi mon thakisiley de, … sir."

"Yes, the Army needs you." I patted him.

Villagers were very happy. Alem's father started crying. He tried to stare at me. He tried to talk to me to tell some sentence to express his gratitude but he could not able to utter a word. But, his sobbing eyes revealed everything. Villagers went back to Anatongre with great relief.

Later on, the Commandant elaborated me the reason behind keeping that room so dark. "Otherwise real NSCN fellow would recognise you and that would be very dangerous for you," he said seriously.

I said, "Thank you so much, sir." But in my inner self I was clear that I didn't care anybody seeing me rescuing a man or not, but nobody should be subjected to that much torture.

However, for Alem it took more than six months to get recovered and to go back to normal life.

20.   Reaching Some Villages of Chandel, Manipur

::

For one of our field programme I was asked to be part of one of the teams to start that programme from New Somtal village of Chandel district of Manipur. I will never forget venturing remote villages of that area, on Indo-Myanmar border, far away from Imphal. We first reached Kakching of Thoubal district for some recess. Kakching town was famous for its rural environment and being rich of fine quality of rice and other vegetables and agro-based economy. The area was self-content. We were invited for lunch by one of our medical officers who was a resident of that place. All the Manipuri dishes prepared by his mother and wife were delicious. I esteemed highly the hospitality and cordiality of the family members. We devoured all those dishes under the caring supervision of the Doctor's mother. She forced us to take more rice, more fishes and more chicken. So after that heavy lunch we left Kakching, seemingly an island in a green sea for its being surrounded by endless paddy field all around extended up to the horizon.

We passed the Pallel market on the way and then after we reached Tengnoupal, a hilly town, from where we took a sub-way towards New Somtal. The main road was heading towards bordering town Moreh, the last habitation of India and huge bordering market on Indo-Myanmar border. And that road ultimately entered in to Myanmar. From Tengnoupal our road towards New Somtal appeared to be rough and tough. Most of the road hardly had any metalled finishing. Our vehicle was simply running on boulders or pebbles of various sizes. Then there was a number of potholes or large or small diggings. Our journey turned into a painful safari. Endless jerking was throwing us from this side to that side and up and down, as if we were on the saddle of some unruly horse. In some places, the road was full of wild water and slippery mud. We were going downwards on that risky hilly track to New Somtal village at the downhill. The whole area, as well as the road was covered with deep forest with a very few localities or villages on the way. After a long struggle, our vehicle took us nearer to the New Somtal and when it was only 5-6 kilometres away, the vehicle was found not in the condition to proceed further. Some of the springs were found broken heavily. So keeping one or two persons with the driver, we started our journey further on foot. The terrain was rocky with a bit of reddish soil. We reached New Somtal village camp with the sun being set in the dusty-red horizon by walking for around 5 km on that unfriendly road after the end of one of the toughest journey.

That village was located in plain land downhill and was surrounded by deep forest rich with teak trees. It was beautiful. Most of the houses were made of wooden planks and thatches or various dry-leaves, with one narrow stream flowing on the southern end. That village was being inhabited by 'Anal-Naga' tribes, people of Sino-Tibetan clan and they were one of the main dominating people of that bordering area of Chandel district. They were also settled on the other side of the Indo-Myanmar border which was hardly a few kilometres away from New Somtal. That area as a whole was the abode of various other tribes such as Moyon, Lamkang, Maring, Paite or Chothe. Some surrounding villages were of people from Kuki or Paite and Lamkang people. The border was simply open and full of the deep forest.

Our camp was found guarded by some youths of Village Volunteer's force, a team of local boys and girls trained in basic security aspects to ensure all necessary assistance to villagers in need. They were very enthusiastic, agile and polite. These youths were trained to cherish and spread the essence of the sense of oneness among all, transcending all diversity, and to dedicate to help each other in time of any emergency or for the sake of this nation. Broken Hindi from their unaccustomed vocal sounded great. I was surprised by hearing those boys and girls try to speak in Hindi, in their own way, in that remote part of Manipur.

The surrounding was full of noise by the cheerful kids and the tweeting of birds back on the trees after a daylong work. But if one remembers the fact that the area was highly infested by various ethnic underground elements, the setting of the sun behind that forest, paving the grimy darkness to set in used to make everybody weird a bit, or to a great extent. That bordering zone was almost safe passage for all such groups for their movement to and from India to Myanmar or vice versa. We passed that night nicely in the care of those hospitable villagers.

After conducting medical and veterinary treatment camp in that village that morning all of our different teams started our journey on foot for other villages on the top of hills around us, keeping our bedding or sleeping bag in our rucksack on our back. With every team, one local volunteer was there as a guide. Villagers were able to talk only in Manipuri other than their mother tongue. So most of us continued communication with the villagers with all possible gesticulation and it was of great joy to make them understood what was in our mind by gesture after a course of genuine struggle by both the party. Elders were found immensely happy once they realised that we made out what they wanted to explain. They used to laugh a lot, so were we!

Thus after visiting about eight villages on the hill, in the forest on various ridges of that hilly terrine our team reached at Tengnoupal after three days. It was a wonderful experience! It was unforgettable. We covered two Kuki villages and one Lamkhing village as well. Everywhere, we were greeted with honest warmth despite all adversity and poverty of those villagers. They treated us as their guest and their hospitality made us overwhelmed. They extended all support to us to make our work smooth and successful. All our teams met there at Tengnoupal that day and we had a closing ceremony there hosted by the locals. We witnessed traditional dances by dance group of Anal, Meitei, Lamkang and Kuki people. The occasion turned into the centre for traditional acumen for a different ethnic culture of Manipur.

We then proceeded to Moreh town, a bordering business hub of Manipur, towards further east from Tengnoupal. I was, or rather we were surprised to see that town, about 130 km away from Imphal, on Indo- Myanmar border. It was a cosmopolitan, though a very small town. It was a little India, a home for people from every corner of this country, where the hilly ranges in Indian side leaned to merge with a near plain piece of land which further extended towards the plain of Myanmar. Other than the township of Moreh in India and market or residential area of Tamu town of Myanmer the whole area was covered with deep forest either in Indian side or in Myanmar side.

In Moreh, one could see Meitei, Naga, Tamil, Assamese, Nepali, Kuki, Burmese, Bihari, Bengalies, Telegu, Marwari or Punjabi were living together and dealing with various sort of business. Local Manipuries such as Meiteis, Nagas or Kukis were mostly farmers. Others were mostly found running shops for selling foreign goods brought from Myanmar. That busy town was consequently the centre for various cultural identities and for educational institutes for children of those businessmen from different communities and linguistics. One could get types of cuisines or restaurants there. From Manipuri or Naga or Burmese dishes to Idli, Dhosa, Chapati, Biriyani or Mogalai, all were found available and were in demand there. These people from different parts of India were residing there since long and some generations of them passed their life in Moreh. People were found in ease with most of the major Indian languages. I was surprised watching a Tamil person talking with fluency in Manipuri, Hindi, Bengali, Assamese, Nepali or even in Burmese while attending customers at the same time.

One narrow river, passing by the eastern side of Moreh town, was demarcating the border in between India and Myanmar. A steel girder bridge, known as 'Indo-Burma Friendship Bridge' on that river was paving the passage to our national Highway-39 to enter into that neighbouring country. The nearest town of Myanmar was a small business hub, mainly of foreign goods, namely 'Tamu' was about 5 km away from that bridge. Comparing the traffic rules in India with that of in Myanmar, it was seen that 'left' was not 'right' there. Once on the road one must take the right side of the road for proceeding ahead. Any Indian driver could be confused easily while driving in Myanmar.

Tamu was a nice town on the valley surrounded by forests, full of wooden or bamboo-made beautiful houses. It was as stunning as a perfect drawing by any renowned artist. All those houses and roads were clean and nicely decorated with flora on the ground or on the vase. Roadsides were found to be home of nicely adorned bamboo-made shops. People, male or female, wearing typical shirts or blouses and lungi with ever-smiling face were in every corner to greet all. Males preferred to have puffs of long "bidis", a sort of local cigarette with bamboo or leaf made beautiful hats on their heads. That busy Tamu market was full of foreign-productions from electronics to clothing from China, Korea, Thailand, Japan, Srilanka and many other countries and items such as wrist watch, television, fridge, camera, sound system, shoes, liquors etc were sold there at simply unbelievable cheap price. Liquors were being sold just like vegetables from temporary roadside shops.

The main road was full of horses or mule carts, rickshaws, jeeps or taxis, with the driver shouting 'Moley'... 'Moley' to invite the passengers. People in Myanmar side were found to pronounce 'Moreh' typically resulting it to be sounded as 'Moley!' However for every 'r' they used to utter 'l'. Visitors from India were coming back with huge such goods to this side without least checking by police of either sides. Those items were then loaded on the vehicles towards Imphal. We halted that night at Moreh. The business places remained busy until late in the evening. All most every community had their church, temple or mosque there and every such worshipping place was found well-maintained and well attended.

We left Moreh early in the morning for Imphal again by going up and up till we reached Tengnoupal and then our journey became mostly downwards up to Imphal valley. But it was a real pleasure visiting Moreh, which deserved to have more care and support to be a bordering trade centre of eastern India. The town and surrounding places were in need to have a business centre in that furthest bordering area which might bring better economic prospects and multiple employment options, in the area from Imphal to Moreh as a whole, directly or indirectly.

21.   Few Hours Near Floating Islands, the Real Wonder

::

That journey to New Somtal and Moreh brought an unexpected ambit for me to visit Loktak Lake, the wonder created by nature by her own hand, perhaps, a place I had been longing to see by my own eyes. Actually, in my initial days in Imphal I was always discouraged from going to that place on the pretext of disturbance due to activities by underground elements. Moreover, I wanted to have some company to have a trip to that heavenly place, about only 45 kilometres away from Imphal, but I could not have any one to give me company. So I could not manage to visit Loktak, though I had enough leisure while staying in Imphal.

Hence, on that occasion, when my teammates conceded to have a tour of the lake, I became so happy, as if I had gotten a lottery. I could not have the patience to reach the place, the aquatic wonder. So, we started for the lake near Moirang town under Bishnupur district. I had an exclusive conception of that lake in mind since I read about that floating lake, but reaching there I discovered that the lake was more beautiful than what was there in my mind, but I did not regret it. The beauty of the area was simply beyond description for me. It seemed part of my dreamland was created by using only green under the blue sky. Olive green water of that huge lake hosting numerous deep green islands was surrounded by high, and not-so-high, green hills, vegetation and forest. It was a different world to make everybody spellbound.

All those islands were actually floating on the water, like a boat. The mysterious whim or wish of the nature that all the organic left-outs, heterogeneous mass of vegetation, soil, decomposed or decayed corpse of flora-fauna had turned into the shape of islands after passing through various phases of cycle. These unique islands were called 'Phumdis'. Those 'Phumdis' were in various size and shape, but mostly were in round shapes and most of those round 'Phumdis' were artificially shaped for creating fisheries. Those round-shaped islands were called 'athaphums'. Literally 'Loktak' denoted 'the end of stream' as the vast lake looked like a bay. It was a water-body where a number of rivers met after their journey throughout the northern part of Manipur and a few also originated from the southern zone of the lake. The southern end of the lake was also hosting the famous "Kebui Lamjao National Park" a safe home to 'brown antlered deer' or 'Sangai', python, sambar, hornbill, gibbon and various other wild species. Though we did not visit that park, it was enthralling to be so near to that forest.

Loktak: House for floating islands

No doubt in the far past this area was nature's own land. But gradually it was ventured by men. Initially a few hamlets of people around the lake were blessed by the natural wealth including fertile soil and fishes from the sweet water. But gradually, the venturing of people increased in and around the lake, in the forest and even into the 'Phumdis' which caused an enormous change in the area. For their livelihood, people started pisciculture by creating tiny fishery ponds on those 'Phumdis' and most of those 'Phumdis' had actually become a farmhouse or fisheries, floating on the water. We were watching those floating ponds. The economy of that vast area under Bishenpur district of Manipur was solely based on the Loktak Lake. Markets, as well as all fish-loving folks in Imphal and other major towns were mostly depended on supply of fish from that lake. Fertile land on 'phumdis' and beyond was very supportive to produce huge crops and vegetables. But, all those compelled the lake, as well as the natural beauty or unique feature of that area, to come to compromise many odds with the environmental balance.

However, the assortment of water and numbers of hills raising heads from that green water, scattered floating islands, hills and forest all most all around that lake was worth consuming through our eyes. It was a completely different experience. One just continued to be absorbed and submitted amazedly before the majestic beauty of nature there.

In the very core of my heart, I found a huge green lotus in that whole sphere or adjacent vicinity of the lake. Those green hills with their heads rose from the green water and those green floating islands looked like the shape of petals of green water lily, floating elegantly on the water that was surrounded by green background of forest, paddy field and forest-covered hills extended far beyond the reach of our eyesight. Through another vision, Loktak was representing the unique essence of 'unity in diversity' of our sovereign country. Those 'phumdis' were like different states which all together made the totality of this nation possible despite apparent diversity which actually to remain as the driving force to keep us united.

Local fishermen were busy in fishing by netting from that deep water by riding on their tiny boats or homemade rafts very much became part of the nature there. Women and men from surrounding villages were doing cultivation work on their respective 'phumdis'. Some of the bigger islands, namely Sendra, Ithing or Thanga, had been changed into resorts to attract tourists. We could not manage to halt there for night but I wished if I could stay at least one night on that magic-island. We went up very close to Sendra and felt greedy. It was obvious that the area, rich of usual and unusual natural beauty, was ready enough to emerge as the most preferred tourist place of India. So that short tour of mine to Loktak was full of joy and adventure.

22.

In the Hub of NSCN

After having lunch bit early that day I set off, along with my local assistant Lipong, for Kisetong village, around 20 km away on the other side of the sky-high hill of Singrep. I planned to reach Kisetong next morning after staying at Amhator village for that night. We kept on walking upwards to reach the peak of the precipice, where Singrep village was situated. By lending an ear to the all-round colloquial of various species of birds coming back after their outing to their nests or nightly shelters on tall trees on our way, we reached near Amhator village when it was almost evening.

It was one of the best fusions of sound and light, as tweeting by birds merging with laughing by villagers coming back to their home, and daylight transforming into twilight. On the other hand, forest-green was coalescing with a blackish backdrop of the forthcoming evening to be followed by dark night. Villagers were returning exhausted from their farm downhill with honest smile to greet us though I was not known to them, none of them missed to bid well wishes either in words or in gesture with their bright and vocal eyes.

Anyway I was too tired but I ultimately reached the playground of Amhator village in the dusk having the sun already set behind the hill of Sitimi area inviting the evening to set in to pervade the time and remaining radiance of the day with its soft darkness. I was rejuvenating myself by merging my sense in the peace of that moment and by cherishing the joy of my being successful to arrive at the village trampling all physical fatigue.

But that good feeling did not sustain for long, as all of a sudden I found a group of men standing in a single-line in that playground, a few metres away from us, just like the conventional army. In that mist of the fast-disappearing daylight, I discovered all those men, were actually youth in camouflaged uniforms and with lethal arms attending roll call in single file formation to inspect the arms and ammunitions. I was sure that they were armed-cadres of an underground organisation.

Lipong whispered in my ear, "Sir, NSCN (IM)." Those boys were giving an OK report to their in-charge about their health and their arms. Though I was struggling to defeat all my sense of fear, I was stunned seeing those disciplined troupes were in perfect order to carry out their routine work. They did not pay least attention to two of us. Actually, it was the guard at distance or OP (observation post) of the group who might have failed to distinguish us entering in to the village in that dusk along with the group of villagers coming back from their field. However, that was the first time I saw the NSCN (IM) group equipped with arms from such a close distance. I observed in every corner of the village, on all the higher platforms, such as rock or roof, there were armed boys guarding the village. We stepped in the house of the village council chairman. He welcomed us without any hesitation. As usual, I was brought to the kitchen of his house which seemed to be the actual drawing room in rural Nagaland.

I was offered a cup of strong tea, rich with milk, sugar and tealeaves. At that time, I was really in need of such a strong drink. I was much relieved after some sips. The chairman informed that NSCN (IM) group reached there that morning only and the village would be their village-base for a few days. He did not reveal anything more about the group and we continued talking about many other issues and happenings.

That very moment, four of the NSCN boys entered there escorting their captain. The handsome and smart young man in full combat uniform and armed with AK-47 came forward and greeted me, "Hi, I'm Shimrey."

I acknowledged his impressive, amiable but tough gesture with sincerity. I was told to give briefs of our activities in and around Kiphire and the reason behind my coming there on that day. We talked in length and I replied all his queries confidently and convincingly. I was told by Captain Shimrey that the village will be under their command as long the base would not be shifted to another place. The villagers ought to abide by the order and norms of the said group for security reasons. No case of disorderliness or indiscipline will be allowed or tolerated and no undue movement of people other than villagers of Amhator will be allowed.

He also ensured that as I was the guest of that village all care will be taken for my comfort staying there provided I cherished no ill motive towards that group. We wished 'good night' to each other and the captain left for that night. Chairman stated that there will be no case of indiscipline or case of consuming foreign liquor by any of the villagers during the camping of the underground group in that village. Everything will be in order as long that group would remain there.

Then we dined there. I went through all my favourite Naga dishes. We continued talking. Actually, I continued listening for long after dinner and after a while, we took black tea. We then prayed to God, for good luck and good health for all before going to sleep. I slept to the deepest and got up at about 4 O'clock in the morning so that we could start our journey to Kisetong village early. I found that there was electricity available at that odd hour to facilitate us with very dim light, though in the previous evening, there was no power supply in the village and I was surprised to find an NSCN man in full uniform and with arms covering his face with a black cloth standing outside, almost on the door.

I was stunned and said after a gape, "Good morning." He said, "Good morning, uthichhey sir (You have left your bed)!" I Said, "Hoi." I came out of the room for going to the washroom.

I came back from the washroom. He was still there. I realised that the whole night I was under watch or guard. I was getting ready but I felt that the guard was bit distracted or as if he wanted to say something! He was almost on the door, and he was watching all my movement.

I invited him inside the room, "Vitorte ahibi na (Please come inside)."

He came in after a few seconds. I greeted him with smile, "Bohibi (Please be seated)." He uncovered long black cloth from his face; he was just a teenage boy. He was hardly 16 or 17 years old. He did not take any seat. I initiated the conversation. He introduced himself as Ashaba. The hard-built boy started talking in a low voice. He was a school dropout from Natsumi village of Seyocheng area. He left school three years back when he was in class eight. He stated that he joined NSCN (IM) for 'nation-work'.

"Ghortey beshi dookh thakisey! Schooltey Pariboley bhi beshi digdar thaka pora, sathikhan logotey nation kaam koriboley mon hoa pora, yaatey join hoi jaisey de. (Ours was a very poor family! It became very difficult for me to continue studying so I joined this group along with friends to work for nation building.)," said the tender warrior.

He stated that all the boys who joined the group were given training in weapon handling and exclusive firing in an unknown place, in a forest far away from the Saramati peak. Usually they were allowed to stay in their native village, with their family, for one month in a year. They were being given free ration and clothing by the group. Sometimes, boys like him were given Rs. 1000/- to Rs. 2000/- as allowance after successful major operations. They were also given up to Rs. 2000/- as grant during X-mas. It was amazing to talk to him, who was dreaming an unknown dream. I was surprised to realise the level of motivation that the boy loved to work for the group and was eager to sacrifice everything for the betterment of the Naga people.

Just before leaving, as till nobody else was there, the boy told that since a few days he did not have any money with him. As he had some urgent need he requested if I could lend him 50 rupees.

"Apuni logotey thakiley 50 rupees dibi na, sir! Kiba urgent kaam thakisey, ami logotey poisa na thaka hoisey de sir."

It was an honest confession or declaration; it was neither begging nor proposal. It was as if the younger brother was apprising about his hardship to his elder brother with confidence that he will definitely be getting all support. However, it was one of the most astonishing and unforgettable moment for me that a man armed with AK-47 and chain of grenade was requesting for Rs. 50/-. I smiled to acknowledge the simplicity and wisdom of the boy, so-called rebel. He promised that he would definitely pay back that amount during X-mas the merriest and jubilant festive time of Nagaland, after getting his X-mas allowance.

As at that moment I did not have change to offer him Rs.50/-, I gave him a currency-note of Rs.100/-. I apologised, "Sorry Bhaitee (brother), I don't have change." I wished him Merry Christmas in advance, and blessed him and wished very prosperous and long life for him in my mind.

Then Lipong came and we departed from the young NSCN man. It took hardly two hours for us to reach Kisetong village before the sun got in its full swing to transpire heat. This Sangtam village, as a whole, was mostly on the lap of the hill and was having a very small patch of land, which could be referred as plain land, required for easy habitation or developing playgrounds. The village was found poorer in shape, and look, in comparison to some other neighbouring villages. Only a few narrow patches of land were found available for common use as village-road or field or yard. Only a very few RCC constructions, including the small church, were there till that time. But the village was rich, very rich of warm hearts and laborious people, who never surrendered before all misfortune.

The way they accepted a new comer like me in their village without any sort of overture was worth cherishing and learning. I roamed through all corner of that real needy village with the Chairman and Gaon buras. Most of the houses were made of either thatch or wood. The want of basic hygiene and sanitation aspects was felt in large. Anybody could feel sad by seeing the helplessness of the villagers. Nowhere one could find any sign that the government did anything for the villagers. One could easily realise that in the village, only a few either infants or elders, were in good health and some of them seemed suffering from some sort of physical deformity.

I was told that such needy villages were not getting the least support from the apathetic administration. Government aids or development project had hardly reached this village. There was no good government school or health centre around. Till that time, as there was no vehicle service available to go to Kiphire, those village people suffered or perished their entire physical and medical problem silently. They were surviving there solely depending on the power of their courage and mental attachment with the soil and, to some extent, due to ignorance and unawareness about the progress in the other zone.

The mark of struggle and poverty was all around. No drinking water source was there nearby. People were found struggling there for drinking water, for agricultural work, for education for their children or even in some cases for all time meals for their kids. Deprivation was so enormous that those people agreed to consider all hardship as natural. They seemed had no idea or had erased most of the gettable or least amenities or minimum requirements from the list of their preview of fundamental rights and tried to be happy by forgetting or sneaking what they were not provided by the government.

In the evening, we came back to Amhator village and stayed there again for the night. That night I had a long discussion again with Captain Shimrey. We again discussed our agenda. I felt as if we were playing chess mentally. He was offensive and I was enjoying defending myself. At the end of the game we seemed pleased with each other, though it was obvious that only the tip of the iceberg was unveiled by each of us. Then again, I passed the night there with one arm-guard outside the room.

23.   Durga Puja at Kiphire Town

Some friends of mine in Kiphire, who were from other states such as Assam, West Bengal, Bihar, U.P., Kerala or Rajashthan, and had come there for service or business decided to organise "Durgapuja" at Kiphire that year. People from different religions and faith such as Christians, Hindus, Muslims or Jains all opined that we could have some festive atmosphere during the puja duration in Kiphire town. But, there were a few doubts among some of the friends about whether people will participate and support, or not? As the political scenario (actually enmity among Assam Rifles and two underground rival groups) could seemingly emerge as the strongest hindrance for such public occasion at that point of time, and it was actually the reason that nobody tried to observe puja in public in the past. I was entrusted with the task of ensuring that there would be consent from all sides towards our effort. All the major local bodies were contacted and convinced that neither any act of indiscipline nor anything that would create the least ill feeling or discomfort to anybody would be allowed. We decided not to allow anybody to use even crackers, as it was apparently not advisable and would not be wise. Even the underground organisations consented that there would not be any objection to let people observe religious festivals.

The local leaders and dignitaries were taken into confidence and all happily agreed to support us. No local was against organising the festival. So we realised that we were, indeed, under the influence of some wrong perception about the place and its people. All the locals were there with us, directly or indirectly, zealously supporting us. So we constituted the puja committee and started preparing for the grand gala. All the locals and non-locals, whom we approached for contribution or donation, irrespective of their religious identity, rendered monetary help happily. To our utter surprise, on the day one of our collection, we managed to get about Rs. 15,000/- within two or three hours. The Hindus, Christians and Muslims, all wanted to have an atmosphere of festivity in Kiphire. So there was no dearth of funds, will and enthusiasm to have the blissful occasion there. We sent our team to Dimapur for marketing. One local businessperson provided his truck to bring the idol of Devi Durga and other requirements, including the Purohit (priest) and Dhaak (Drum) with the drummer, from Dimapur.

Finally, it took the shape of a gala of joy. Children from all over the town and its outskirts were there in the beautiful pandal all day and evening over all three days. I could not remember about the rituals but the cheers, joy and sense of freedom from the tension among people, especially among kids, really made our toil worthy. Most of the residents relished 'Khichdi' (type of hotchpotch) and Labra (mixed vegetable) there, as community lunch was prepared on all three days.

In that pretext people, like me, who were far away from their home and kin even during that festival, got real joy and a fair chance to recompense grievances for not being able to be with family at our native places. All over those three days, there were cultural programmes, singing, recitations and dance competitions for kids and ladies.

After the puja, as some unspent money was left with the puja committee it was unanimously decided to purchase a good set of cricket gear. So, good numbers of balls, bats, wickets, pads, batting gloves, keeping gloves, guards and many other essentials were bought and brought from Dimapur. Local youths were found very enthusiastic to have such kits. Though local boys were hardly found playing cricket but on the ground they were found to be very well in batting, bowling and fielding. All of them had tremendous adaptability. They had the instinct to learn very fast. So, the craze of cricket stepped in Kiphire. Every day, youngsters including some jawans of Assam Rifles used to gather in the afternoon at the playground just beside the Assam Rifles camp. Some of the boys I knew were very good cricketers and were actually a hardcore cadre of underground organisations. They were gentle, courteous and jolly. Whenever they were deployed occasionally, at Kiphire they used to come to practice or play with us in the afternoon and after the darkness set in the night, they used to be on duty in their combat dress with arms in their hand. If they could manage, they used to come again next afternoon to play with us. Very often, it happened that in a friendly match, the batsman used to be a jawan of Assam Rifles and the one at the non-strikers end was an underground boy.

24.

The Boldest Tea

O nce we halted at Amhator village for the night to visit the villages, Kior and Changchor the next day. So we started for the villages in the morning by our vehicle number NLP-11.Yes vehicle number NLP-11, the most popular vehicle for the people in Kiphire area. Actually, people jokingly referred to their legs as vehicle number NLP-11. They used to mock the government in that way. As there was no vehicle or conveyance provided for village folk in the remotes, so common people were solely dependent on their feet or NLP-11.

In contrary to other surrounding villages these two villages were located quite down in the foothills. So the three of us, Lipong, Hukhato and I were walking in ease by seeing various trees, birds and flowers. We came across fowls and many unknown birds several times. The forest road was through the bushes of emblic or 'amla' and other small trees or bamboos. The kutcha road was covered with dried leaves, which were very dangerous in such a dry season, but at that very moment, those leaves were making the journey full of interesting rustle and every step to drop on a soft surface. A little ignition from matchstick, cigarette or bidi or any such litter could cause a fire within a moment, and due to paucity or want of water, taming such fire became very difficult and very often it turned into a devastating forest-fire.

After a few kilometres, we reached at the Forest Bit Office compound, consisting of an office building and four small quarters like RCC structures, where only a forest guard was found available. The guard was staying with his family in a quarter. All those old quarters were in a ruined condition. No other family or nobody else was staying in the area of within 3-4 kilometres of that place. The forest guard was having two small kids, one daughter and one son. That family was also expecting their third child. The man talked to us and offered a warm place in his room, as well as in his heart, to take rest for a while. His wife came there to greet us. She was seemingly in the most critical stage of pregnancy. She talked to us and offered us tea without the least vexation.

She was confident that she will have no problem in giving birth to their new "gift of God", as she termed her child in her womb, in that home away from any hospital, doctor or maid or any other people. She was proud to state that her two other children came to this world in the same way in that lonely place. I felt pity for the compulsion and helplessness of that mother but her guts and strength were worth admiring. However, that happy family was found in a world exclusively of their own and away from any intrusion.

We further proceeded to Kior and Changchor. First, we reached Kior village and I met the Village Council

Chairmen, the village elders. We had a grand lunch at the village in the house of the chairman. Then we proceeded to Changchor village and as the road was through almost a plain terrain, we walked in ease. Both the villages were surrounded by deep forests. As those were located down the hill, the villagers had water resources nearby and their farms were also near to the habitation. There were a few fisheries or pond, and they had a lot of ducks, which was quite atypical in such villages. The village was rich with plenty of trees of various fruits such as mangoes, guavas, peaches and a few apple trees. We had a nice time there in those villages as we had long interaction with youths.

We started our return journey early in the afternoon. Then we reached the same Forest Bit Office late in the afternoon. The forest guard came running with a full smile. He said in joy, "Sir, amakhan Ishwar morom pora bachcha paise de. Chhukri paisey. (By the grace of the God we have got one more child, we have been blessed with a baby girl.)".

His wife gave birth to the baby about two hours back. Actually, I was the first person with whom he shared his happiness after seeing the face of his just born daughter. He compelled us to step in his quarter again. I could hear the cheer and joy from the bedroom where his two other children and wife were trying to talk to the baby.

After a while, his wife, though looking exhausted, came to us smiling and shared her contentment with us. She then went inside and within a few minutes, she was back with hot tea for us. I was surprised at seeing the woman who gave birth to a baby two hours back, without a nurse or any other help, was walking and working. She even prepared tea for us. It was really beyond my imagination. I esteemed her will, strength and confidence highly. Only enormous mental power could make a woman recover so fast after delivery without any support of any doctor, nurse or any other woman. It was near impossible for me to believe that throughout all those phases, full of pain and more pain, only her husband and two helpless children were there beside her in that vicinity. She stood as an epitome of courage in my eyes.

I thanked God for taking care of the mother and the baby. I saw the baby, with pink lips, pink palms and silky hair, sleeping happily. Then I had a sip of the tea, the boldest tea, I must say, I had tasted ever in my life. I had every sip of that tea to honour the great woman. The tea was full of inspiration.

25.   Trip to Jalukie~Peren

I heard much hearsay about Jalukie and Peren area from people in our office and out of the office. Jalukie or Peren was like this or like that! There, underground cadres were roaming in the open! They were openly extorting! The area was witnessing confrontation, involving an exchange of fire almost regularly… Non-locals were unsafe there! So I, or anybody else, was never encouraged to go to that area. So that area was always veiled to me. Very often, I passed the Kukidolong village area while coming from Dimapur to Kohima, from where the road towards Jalukie or Peren took its own way towards the west. While coming from Dimapur after crossing Meziphema the road towards Jalukie through a hilly range covered with deep forest after crossing the bridge on the Chathe river near Kukidolong had been a spectacleof great curiosity. Watching that hilly terrain under veil of the blackish-green deep forest on the other side of the river had always been sensational to me.

Once I was told to visit that area for contacting some village authorities. So I set out for Jalukie on one fine morning from Kohima. After crossing that bridge near

Kukidolong, I found that we were almost in the grab of the forest. Those huge trees mostly leaned on the road to make even the sunrays not to shine the road in some area. The whole area was under Peren sub-division of the Kohima district. It was a very less populated area. Zelieng, Kuki, Liangmai or Rongmai were the major tribes of Peren sub-division. There were less numbers of villagers or vehicles that we came across on the road, but we found numbers of army-vehicles mostly going to Dimapur.

The road was narrow but it was in a very good condition, and so I reached Jalukie soon, where I got the company of a Zelieng boy as a guide. The town looked like a little valley, and was busy in its own rhythm just like other places. Markets and shops were full of restless people. Most of the shops were being run by non-locals. All were polite and happy. I found nothing odd about the area and I liked the atmosphere there. We took tea in a hotel there and after that I met some administrative officers to seek help to open our office there. Then we proceeded further for Jalukie 'B' village away from the town. It was a Zelieng village, from where the undulating valley started extending itself to get merged with the hilly-forest area of Assam. I met the village council chairman and other gaonburas there. We passed a cheerful evening followed by a peaceful night.

Peren area as a whole was a bit isolated, for being far away from big cities, and for its being on tough terrain, to add with it was adjacent to a remote part of Assam such as Karbi-Along or Haflong and near to border with Manipur. Consequently, Jalukie and Peren were preferred by all extremist groups active in Assam, Manipur, Nagaland or other regions for affording free passage for their movement or transition from one place to another place. Local people had no other options other than witnessing and affording possible assistance to those groups passing through that area in huge numbers equipped with heavy arms every now and then. Locals were consequently busy witnessing the segments of brawny domination by either the underground groups or the armed force, despite all adversity. Hence the economy of this area never ever witnessed any remarkable pace towards prosperity.

Despite all those doldrums, the people here were found to defeat all pessimism and to lead life happily. They were absolutely hospitable and helpful to all, including non-locals, without being biased. During those 3-4 days I never witnessed the least incident of what I was told earlier. With Kabbu, the Zelieng boy as a guide, I visited various Zelieng, Kuki and Rongmai villages, such as Maikham, Samzuram, Dunki, Athibong, Punglanwa etc. and everywhere I was welcomed by the villagers. I talked to elders and youths. Most of the youths, especially from not so well to do families, were worried that they could not expect to continue college education for basic support. They felt bad for their helplessness though they knew that to bring all-round development in that area, and to ensure positive environment to have shielded from any ongoing uncertainty, true education was the most important aspect.

"Amakhan na poriley to dusra manukhan amakhan pora kaam loi thakibo, amakhan ke thogi thakibo! Hoi ..., na nahoi? Hoiley bhi ......? (As long we are not fairly educated we will be continued to be exploited by others. They will keep on fooling us. Is not it? But what can we do?)" One boy stated as an honest realisation on his part.

I really found those youths helpless and confused. Those rural youths actually never imagined a life, a so-called prosperous individual life, where they will not be concerned about the prosperity or happiness of their community. Hence the sense of helplessness, that they may fail to do good for their village or their people in the days to come, might have made them depressed. They were in need of support, a true leader or inspiring figure to lead their zeal and vigour in the right direction and to make them realise that only eruditely strong individuals could make the community or own people strong enough to fight all adversity.

Fertile lands there in those villages were found hosting hale and hearty paddy, corns or types of fruits. Most of the people had good numbers of livestock, piggery or fisheries. Rearing pigs or goats brought them good economic support as traders were taking huge numbers of those products to market at Dimapur or Kohima regularly. People from different communities were also living there by maintaining absolute harmony.

The next day, we went to Peren town, far away from Jalukie. It was the sub-divisional headquarters. We met some officials there for guidance about how to approach village heads for our work. We then visited Peren a nearby village, talked to the village head, and got a warm response from the villagers. The youth were especially very enthusiastic to have village-level training there. But the evening used to arrive with some sort of gloom in the Peren-Jalukie area. All the shops were found closed by the evening and the movement of people on the roads was very less. It was due to circumspection of people to avoid the least confrontation with armed forces, such as the Army or Assam Rifles, or with the underground groups who used to appear without any prior notice. People were not at all comfortable in coming out of their houses after evening hour. The bright green forest or huge field or kheti of 7-8 feet tall corn, which looked lively and dazzling in the daylight used to turn into an awful black, enough to threaten anybody imagining that anybody could come out jumping from those bushes, jungle or corn-fields with lethal arms in hand. But I had not heard about any such incident from anybody there in those days, but unfortunately those perceptions were certainly there in the mind of the people.

So that visit to that area was a sort of lesson to me. It helped me a lot to become disillusioned about any place or people there. I came back to Kohima with immense cheer that I initiated amity with people of that area. We selected two boys from Jalukie-Peren area for a study-tour to New Delhi. After that, I went to Peren and Jalukie on different occasions.

26.   Trekking to Seyocheng Area

I planned to go to Seyocheng area, especially to Sitimi, Yangzitong and Natsumi villages, along with two of our staffs from that area. The ridge on which the villages were situated was clearly visible from the veranda of my room at Kiphire and used to appear as if we could even touch that ridge. The whole area was covered with a dense forest. It was at least 45-55 kilometres away from Kiphire, while going by road via Sanphure area, and trekking through the hills and forest after crossing Singrep the distance may come down to 25-30 kilometres. Hence, for common people, trekking was the only feasible alternative to reach there.

We - Lipong, Khugato and me - started early in the morning so that we could reach Singrep village by climbing up the Singrep peak, the steepest vertical challenge on our way, before the sun started getting hot. We took rest there for a while. In Nagaland, every house in every village was ever ready to host any stranger, tired or otherwise, to ensure arranging all comfort by offering tea or meal or shelter. So no trekking was ever too long or too tiresome. After Singrep, no very steep hills or very tough trekking was there on the way for us till we reach under Seyocheng ridge. We reached Kisetong village comfortably and got ourselves ready for tough trekking ahead up to Sitimi by climbing up and up. It was really challenging due to slippery and rocky track in some patches. My Burmese shoe had a rubber sole, purchased from 'Moreh' in Manipur, it helped me a lot and I did not miss my step for even once. Crossing muddy tracks through the bamboo bush on the steep slope and then slippery, rocky and narrow step by keeping my chest, or sometimes my back, and palms, pressed or rubbed with hill was really challenging. Boys taught and guided me to overcome all those ordeals. They were teaching me how to step forward while walking, rubbing my back with a rocky slope of the hill where just few centimetres away from my foot it was a deep gorge ready to swallow me in its dark hole in case of any little flaw.

But that dark black gorge full with dark grey erupting clouds under my feet gave me the opportunity to witness a divine beauty that I never ever experienced before. To all my surprise, I found a bright and huge rainbow to appear on that grey background from deep of the bottom, away behind the green forest, much below the rock where we were walking. We witnessed the wet canvass of nature brushed with seven heavenly colours causing the rainbow to climb high and higher to reach the far away firmament. It appeared that I was almost top of the rainbow. It was bright sunlight being poured on us as well as on the part of the hill where we were standing, and on the other hand, it was a heavy shower on the hill and forest not very far from us. The hide and seek by darkness and light, by rain from the darkest cloud and clear sky made me speechless. I was overwhelmed by witnessing that blissful whim of nature. At some points of time, some torn black-clouds enabled to cover the part of the sun making the bright, and brighter rays of the sun were emitted in single or multiple scattered rays, as sharp as swords, by perforating clouds to cause a spectacular view for us.

Finally, we reached Sitimi in the evening and saw that the villagers had already returned from their daily cultivation work. Children were running and shouting jovially. Ladies were busy to make all domestic pets such as pigs, hens and other livestock caged in place. It was the time when villagers used to remain very busy.

The village was in the valley, or plateau, on the top of the hill, hence it had larger area as habitation consisting huge area for church, school, number of shops and village roads. Shops were found busy with few customers. One mother was shouting at her kids, girls were gossiping among themselves. It was lively and boisterous. We were approaching Mr. Akheto's house where we supposed to stay. For me, in specific, it was relieving to get into the domestic life after long and tough trekking through a deep jungle and a steep hill.

All of a sudden, we heard the sound of a vehicle coming from the opposite direction away from us. It was a misty dusk. I thought it might be a truck plying for villagers purpose. That vehicle was not far away and I saw that it was a local "Shaktiman", one small truck with tremendous capacity to run in bad or the worst road with a heavy load.

To my utter surprise, villagers were found to become very scared and to give silent attention to the passengers of the truck. Children stopped playing or any sorts of movement or talking and most of them disappeared in their houses with in a moment. There was no other sound other than the "vroom, vroom ..." of that vehicle. We found the vehicle was full of young men, in combat dress and with various types of arms. One person was on the bonnet of the vehicle with an LMG mounted on the top board. We also gave space to that vehicle. It stopped a few metres away just after crossing us. By that time, I found that no villagers were around, all went inside their houses. One of our boys, Khugeto Sema, went near the truck and talked for a while to the person seating on the front seat. I kept on taking everything with ease. The vehicle moved ahead and disappeared in the forest background. Sema came back. It was a troupe of NSCM(IM) on vehicle patrolling as they were camping in their base, nearer to the area, in another village. The commander had enquired about us and about our purpose of coming there.

I got back my normal breath and we proceeded further. The village, and villagers, also came back to life once again. We found elders again gathered in front of the shop and at the gate of the church. Ladies were also going to the church for evening prayer. Normalcy was back. We crossed the beautiful church. People greeted us, "Bhaal achhey (How are you)?" or "Kotjayachhey (Where are you going)?" It was as if we had met several times earlier.

We reached Mr. Akheto's house and exchanged good wishes. We had tea and a long chat and humour. My fatigue left me soon. Villagers were very happy that I took heart to trek long and a tough route for coming to the village. We kept on talking on our ideas and issues on Nagaland, about this country and about the world. Elders were worried about the next generation, especially about educated youths who were not interested in agricultural work or rural life. They were also honestly worried about ongoing deforestation, global warming, various new diseases, less rain, disappearing of water sources, increasing soil erosion, ongoing violence, intolerance and many other burning or silly issues.

At dinner, we enjoyed the buffet sitting all around the fire in the middle of the kitchen. Bowls on small tables were decorated with boiled Laipatta, boiled beans, boiled cabbages, boiled potatoes, chutney (sort of sauce) made of bamboo-shoots, raja-mircha (local chilly), etc and chicken, cooked with no oil, no spices, some salt, chilly, water and nothing else. All dishes were delicious and I considered myself blessed for getting the opportunity to have such tasty food, in such company and in such a place. We stayed in the guest room of the church that night.

The next morning, we visited Natsumi and Yangzitong villages. I had some memorable time to get the glance of rural living of Sema and Sangtam people, and of the natural beauty of Sitimi. One could have a view of Kiphire town from some places of the village.

Only by staying in such a village, could one witness how rural life rolled from dawn to the next dawn! Roosters will make one leave the bed in time. In all his surroundings, he will feel the vibration of life getting ready or warming up for the forthcoming day to utilise the light and energy of the sun in full. Livestock were rushing out of their stables. Dogs were busy too, running and barking, to maintain the line and discipline of those cows or pigs out for grazing in the jungle. Ladies were shouting at their kids or pets and getting ready for marching towards their 'Kheti' or agricultural land. There would be a movement of people in and around the church. The sound of transistor from nearby may reach to sense through ear to give the local or national news.

Every movement of the hands of the wristwatch will make you witness different colours of life. Then there remained idle noon, followed by afternoon, for them who did not go to field or farm. Again, there will be some movement, agility, or wave indicating the life returning home by the end of late afternoon. The rattle of cattle, giggle by women, shrieking by kids, singing loudly by some boys, added with the voice of radio transmitting "Basti Manu Laga Programme (Programme for farmers)" the most beautiful programme for rural people ever broadcasted by the All India Radio, Kohima would be there one by one. There will be volatile lively wave of vim and vigour in shape of gossiping, in shape of singing, in shape of laughing, in shape of reading loudly by kids or in shape of domestic arguments in between family members. Then the silhouette of life will be slowly disappearing before your eyes, into your eyes and senses, when you will be hugged by deep sleep.

27.   GPRN Acknowledged Our Work

For about 45 days I went far away from Nagaland to the Garhwal hill of Himalaya near the 'Trishul' peak to attend some training. Those high hills were covered with pine forests a bit different from the hilly terrain of Nagaland. The Naga hill was rich with a variety of flora and greenery, whereas Garhwal was home for the high and rocky mountain. Two different terrains were hosting two different shades of beauty but both were abode of simple and laborious people with beautiful minds. It was winter so I enjoyed the snowfall every now and then. In between snowfall, it was bright sunlight, or moonlight, making all snow covered peaks or hill to glare as silver-white to spark from every square-inch of those snow. I used to enjoy trekking in the forest and hill with friends equipped with camera and packed-food. Walking on the hill-slope covered with pine-leaves was a big challenge as those leaves made the tracks slippery. We also managed to visit Tehri-dam, Bageshwar, Kosauni, Almora, Nainital and many other places. So it was a long outing for me from Kiphire as I also availed leave to stay at my native for some days on the way back to Nagaland.

Another officer was sent at Kiphire by headquarters to look after the work in my absence. From my native place, I again came to Guwahati and then reached at Dimapur by the night-service bus via Jakhlabandha, where night did not dare to darken the vicinity, following the same known route. Then when I reached at our headquarter at Kohima I was told to proceed to Kiphire immediately as our office there was facing some major crisis. I came to know that a few days back NSCN served a notice to our Kiphire office demanding Rs. 15,000/- as local tax and the payment was to be made on the very next day so we had no time to think over, neither had we any option other than reaching Kiphire immediately by any means.

I reached at Kiphire late in the evening and rushed to all the known dignitaries there who had some access to the higher-ups of the underground. I sought their help to make the NSCN-headquarters convinced that we were functioning there to assist the poor and needy people residing away from the reach of the government machinery or development drive. Through us, the needy villagers could convey their urges to the appropriate end and being a public servant there were no means available with us to manage to spare any fund in that way as was imposed on us. All my friends extended great support and favour towards me. In that night itself, I was taken to a finance official of NSCN, who was present at that very time at Kiphire to look after the work pertaining to collection of such tax, and I tried my best to elaborate our activities and all our pros and cons. There was a long discussion among them in Sangtam language.

At last, it was decided that one messenger from the end of the finance official will be sent to Seyocheng area for a final decision as that official could only propose for exemption for us on the basis of what I had projected. So I was told to wait till the next evening for the final resolution of NSCN. So the messenger left Kiphire for Seyocheng or Sitimi area where some hierarchy of NSCN, who was authorised to take decision on such taxing, was camping at that time in their village-base in Seyocheng.

It was a practice that underground groups used to impose levies on selected individuals or department or business-heads as security-tax to ensure that tax-givers would not be disturbed by the group. Very often, imposing and collecting tax took place clandestinely. People actually came to know, this way or that way, who or which department rendered such tax or not but those givers used to pretend otherwise as if they did not give such tax. There prevailed some games for hiding the facts at the behest of the authority who supposed responsible for ensuring solution of that problematic practice. Ultimately, those amounts were reimbursed from the general public especially from the local poor people. Those businessmen used to hike prices of essential commodities, public servants had their own way to meet the loss, either by giving less output or by claiming service charge in an inconspicuous way. So, general and needy locals were the actual prey.

Nonetheless, I was shocked as by that very time, I continued working at Kiphire area for more than two years and I never faced such a discomfited situation. Somewhere the development brought some thin line of sense of difference or isolation, which was hurting me indeed. It was the first time that I found myself as a non-local in my mind. But, all my friends there and all resourceful dignitaries I approached the previous evening for help stood beside me and ensured me that the problem would be solved. The very next day, I was waiting eagerly for the sun to get set.

So in the evening I rushed with my wise friends again to the finance official, desperately hoping for a favourable response. By that time, the messenger of all my hope was back again from Seyocheng. I was told to be at ease and the man revealed that his esteemed command consented to exempt our office at Kiphire from such taxing. And I was handed over a letter from the Command of NSCN, 'Government of People's Republic of Nagaland' or GPRN, Seyocheng Zone referring to such an exemption. It was truly relieving for me and for my department at that point in time. It was great on the part of higher-ups of GPRN that they understood our limitation and believed our activities worthy for the people of Nagaland. That very letter was sent to Kohima immediately.

I felt bad about myself for indulging in sentiments that saw the wrong perception about people. It was the honest support of my friends that the problem was solved on that occasion. However, I was told that during my absence our Kiphire office somehow failed to remain at ease with the locals, as the officer-in-charge who was sent to look after the work in my absence failed to remain accessible by far for many people there, which might have made his staying at Kiphire mere isolation. As he used to drink to the deepest in the evening, he used to make huge chaos or mess till late in the night, which is not considered a decent way of life in any society. Boys tried their best to make him understand the fact, but unfortunately every evening used to bring same fate for the office and the near surroundings. The notice issued to us by GPRN imposing the tax was actually a result of our being unbecoming and indisciplined to a reasonable extent in their eyes. There were many instances that the guilty in the eyes of NSCN had been considered deserving fatal consequences for breaching the norm to abide by the discipline.

I realised that what people despised most in other people there was indulging in double standards in manner and in conduct. Hush-hush attitude used to push one aloof from the people. I found honesty as the safest policy there. Closed door meetings with specific people were never advisable. One must mix up with all with an open mind. They even did not allow categorising people on the basis of social or official stature. I saw higher officers such as DM or SP take a meal together sharing the same table happily with drivers or guards, in official function or in a social gathering. It is possible only when the men of higher social or official stature are wise enough to realise that all are equal in the eyes of Almighty. We found there the officers and their subordinates maintain relations like members of the same family for instance.

Such experiences helped me to have more friends in every walk of life in Kiphire. Nobody ever denied rendering any possible help to me when I was in need so I learnt to act or react in the same spirit. There was physically enormous adversity or scarcity but no penchant of denial was ever found existing in the mind of the people.

28.   Christmas, the Divine Season

When undiscernibly everything around wasfound to become a source of joy, people, in each corner of Nagaland, found to be happy and content, in true sense and nature seemed changed into a festive mood, it was for sure that Christmas was knocking the door. It was almost impossible to specify or distinguish when and how the festive mood and essence of Christmas set in all over Nagaland. And in Kiphire, for its being a small town, all residents knew each other hence rejoicing and merriment appeared to be manifold in the air. I should say 'December-January' was X-mas season there. How and when it approached and pervaded every inch of Kiphire, I could not manage to realise!

Suddenly we found it was Holy X-mas everywhere. Groups of children were busy rehearsing the gospel in church or garden or any yard for performing finally in the church. In the evening, all rooftops used to get dazzled with huge Christmas stars in numerous lights of different colours during the availability of electricity. However, people who could afford to have a generator used to keep their houses enlightened for long, long hours or throughout the night. The Catholic church covered with lights made us feel delighted and proud. Some boys used to roam around in the attire of Santa Claus. The joy pervaded everywhere as schools remained closed after their final examination. Children were free to cheer.

We all were entranced in the sense that He is somewhere nearer to us, eager to see us doing better for this world, for humankind and doing no harm to anybody. I gathered immense strength by seeing Jesus dedicate himself for serving the people; he was crucified for teaching humans to love and serve others. His compassionate smile on the 'Cross' always glitters my heart. But as I believe that all wise sense within us or in our mind is actually an essence of the Lord and very often we fail to save that Lord in our mind from being crucified by the devil's intentions in our minds. We let the good in our heart be hacked by the bad. It needs immense guts to make the good to win over the bad in our mind. That is why the earth is still witnessing injustice, cruelty or violence. So for me it is inspiring to be lively doing and thinking good for all living beings, as by doing that I can be able to make the essence of the Lord to consider my mind and body as His abode.

Though my room was like a club-house for neighbouring children, but on 24th December night all those kids rushed to my room for performing the gospel. All were either in a new dress, in the guise of Santa, in red coat or jacket, red trouser, red conical cap and with a white beard made of cotton. They sang, danced and invited me for their programme the next day in church. I was very late that night to go to bed. Actually we wished such nights to stay long and longer.

We had arranged a picnic in the room of one of my friends John, from Kerala. I finally could manage to go to bed at about 0130hrs. Soon I placed myself under the quilt to get lost in deep into the embrace of sleep. But, after a few moments I heard a mild rattling sound nearby. It got me awake from my drowsiness. I realised it was not the knock of the forthcoming dream but a real knock, though mild, on my door.

I asked, "Who? Hallo! Who is there?"

There a boyish voice brought the reply, "Ami achhey de, sir (It is me, here, Sir)!"

For me that was enough reply for opening the door. I never bothered who actually that "me" was! But, I was sure that, somewhere, I heard that voice before. I opened the door with a bit dizziness left in me. I found the outer world full of icy moonlight and the sky was so clear that I could even see the Saramati peak sharp. It was baffling. Everything around was silent, the roads were free from any noise as all went for recess for the night. After a long pause, I found a man standing in the shadow of the terrace.

The man, from the shadow, said, "Merry Christmas, sir," and came forward.

He was in a complete combat dress with his face covered with a piece of black cloth and a long-barrelled arm on his back. The sound of his steps in heavy shoes, with metallic-sole smashing the pebble and sand, sounded heavier and terrible. He uncovered his face. I recognised him. He was Ashaba, the NSCN fellow I met long back in the early dawn at Amhator village. He was guarding my room from outside the whole night. He extended his right hand holding a note of one hundred rupees.

He said, "Itu ratitey apuni pora loa taka return diboley aahishey de, sir. (That night I borrowed hundred 'taka' from you. I am here to pay you back.)"

I was so surprised and scared. I recovered and replied, "Keep it with you please. Rakhibi na! It is Christmas."

He smiled, "No, thank you, sir. You helped me a lot. Apuni amikey digdar thaka timetey beshi modat karichhey. Ami Christmas laga allowances pai jaise de sir. (You helped me a lot when I was passing through a tough time. It is Christmas and I have got my allowances.)"

He just held my hand and forced the note into my fist and disappeared saying, "Pichhey log pabo dey (see you)."

I mumbled, "Hoi, hoi, hoi." And I realised that two more fellow cadres came out from the shadow of the guava tree in the yard and disappeared following Ashaba.

I went to sleep again with that note as my Christmas gift. It was really touching. I actually never repented for giving the amount to that boy neither had I kept it in my memory that I rendered any help to him. So I never imagined that I would get that amount back in this way. I realised the fact that there was a vast difference in between getting something and getting something back. Getting something back not only makes that thing precious but also elevates the borrower to a noble height. I saluted his honesty, commitment and high-spirit and prayed to Almighty for his safety and wellbeing.

I woke up late the next morning. It was gospel and the church bell got wild at that moment. I came to the church. It was gorgeously decorated with flowers and tree-branches especially pine, inside the church. There were chains of leaves made of various colours of kite paper fixed all over the fencing, walls and top of the church. Then there was a huge Christmas tree under which children decorated various toys showing how angels came to the stable where Jesus was born to enlighten the world. I entered the church and took a seat.

The Pastor was interpreting the grace of God. I was wondering what to pray? How to pray? Why to pray? I knew He always thought and prayed for others. And I gradually conceived that mind was the actual abode of God. We should never keep our mind away from thinking of Him. Only then can we make our life a blissful journey. The church is actually to guide us to be always attached with God, to lead us to do the right thing in the right way.

My neighbouring aunty came to me smiling. We wished each other. She was looking after cooking in the kitchen of the church that auspicious day to prepare for a grand-community-lunch. She was really busy even then she told me, "Malik apunito 'paan' na khai. Cigarette na khai. 'Modhu' vi na khai. Apuni hoccha Christian achhey de! You are a true Christian."

She gave me a tiny cross made of steel and fixed it with my silver-chain on my chest with her own hand and said, "Keep it with you. It will always save you." She prayed for me in Sangtam language keeping her eyes closed and rushed to the kitchen. I do not smoke, drink or take 'paan' for nothing but just out of commitment to my inner self. I felt blessed that I was given the holy cross in that way. I started realising His presence nearer to my heart, nearer to my inner self. I knew and I was confident that, whether I realised or not, 'He' came to guide me and save me on several occasions.

29. Mysterious Pungro and Zinky, Darling of Kiphire

If one looked down from Kiphire town, their sight will fall on a tiny river with yellowish sand bank on both sides. It was 'Zinky' nala, actually 'Zinky' river, the only major passage carrying water in this area. Though, it became wider, stronger and more whimsical in rainy season for being affluent of muddy water and looked greyish black from above. In rainy season, the river was to drain all the rainwater coming down from hills around, washing the forest with a huge force dragging even the big trees or rock or boulders on its way. Hence, the river water was found carrying huge or small logs or trees. Every drop of rain in the Kiphire area was found rushing down, after touching the ground, to 'Zinky' frenziedly. That time it was very risky to go in to river because you never knew that you could be struck by a heavy tree or any log of wood any time.

Otherwise, it was as blue as glittering eyes. From above it looked like a browse of brush, by perfect hand, with blue colour in yellowish background with dots of some other colours scattered on it to show pieces of many white and a few black or grey boulders here and there. The area on the river bed near the Zinky-bridge was awesome. It was the wild river running on glittering boulders there, surrounded by all-round greenery. Seemingly, as if it were a play zone for uncanny mermaid of any fable. I believed in full moonlight one could definitely find mermaids playing there and taking moon-bath on the large milk-white boulder on the blue water of 'Zinky'. Some local storyline beckoned that even not long back the river used to carry gold with its sand.

Very often, I wished to talk with the restless 'Zinky', as it used to drag out the poet within. One need not be worried who is listening or who will say what? But bringing out precious words to acknowledge the beauty of the river of that river bed, of that greenery or of that solitude seems to be natural or spontaneous for any human being. I did not care if that appeared to be bearing no sense. So my course of conversing very often dared to take the shape of a verse:

Don't you know that you don't know?

Where are you coming from?

May be from the core of a rock or from the ecstasy

You fall to drift us with your restlessness.

Like the princess you dare pleasantly

To discount, all on the way.

In rain wild and babbling you embrace all on brims

Or beyond, as a must elephant lifting woods

To float with fast muddy water to menace me and all.

In autumn, a tame you look adorable.

You teach us to be in love with the earth.

Greedy leaves of cane or nameless trees lean

To touch you to flirt on pretty pretexts.

You try to make all to listen your songs.

The melody gives ears ease and soul a peace.

Spring makes a shy you to rest singing.

Jingling you submit to help all, to invite people

To be with you all the day so bright.

Moon beams glitter on you whole night.

Day remain shiny and breezy around you,

As you smear all blue of the firmament.

You live long, flow far long, hailing life everywhere

Teach people to live happy life,

Using life in the best way to make all agile.

Blow away all ill in us, making us smile.

In spring and in summer, the bed of 'Zinky' used to become the favourite destination for picnic goers. Even during acute water scarcity up on the top of the hills people from Kiphire town and surrounding villages used to go down to 'Zinky' for washing their cloths or for taking a bath.

Summer really used to bring serious scarcity of water all over Kiphire, women and kids remained busy on their toes in search of little water as normal water supply used to become very irregular. Sometimes we could not get water supply for days and in that situation we used to purchase water from wagers who used to bring water from far away streams and sell at Rs. 10/- or Rs. 15/- per bucket. So in those dire days we used to spend more Rs. 15/- for having a minimal bath. Coincidently in Sangtam language 'Ki' stands for 'water'. So people used to ridicule that the name 'Kiphire' actually denoted 'Ki is free' or 'water is free'.

"But Kiphire is actually 'water-free' or 'where there is no water'", people used to add, especially in summer.

So they jokingly suggested that the actual name of 'Kiphire' should have been 'Ki malley' meaning 'no water', as in Sangtam 'malley' denoted 'not available'.

Hence that river was of great significance for Kiphire throughout the year. One could search there for delicious trout fish too. 'Zinky' was the darling in the eyes of one and all in Kiphire. In quite a few occasions, I also ventured in to 'Zinky' though I knew coming back to my room by climbing the steep and long slope of the hill would be very sweaty. My little friend Zezi from my neighbourhood used to accompany me almost everywhere like my shadow. He was in class-VII, very intelligent and used to take a keen interest in everything in the world except his studies. For describing his activities, I would be in need to pen down another book. We took a bath in clean blue water of 'Zinky' more than once, as we used to go down there with roasted corn or biscuits. Zezi used to come down heavily on the apparently calm water by throwing his body into it and tried his best to swim in waist deep water, splashing water in all directions.

Zinkey river: appeared to house mermaids

Some times when there was no one else around, he used to throw out even his brief and enjoy running and rolling on the sand in joy with his creamy white body, to get his body coated with sand, and then jumped in to the water. Then he used to sit on the milk-white boulder just in the middle of the river, which was supposed to be occupied by the mermaid in the night of the full moon. The golden-haired and blue-eyed boy used to glaze in the dazzled sunbeam to make the moment heavenly.

All of a sudden, out of obsession or illusion, I used to get myself sitting on the clean pebbles in the clean blue water of the river, having two sides covered with golden sand. Those gold dusts made Zezi's body gold plated. In that world of fancy Zezi kept on laughing, running and jumping around me and at a short distance many of those mermaids were basking on the gold dust spreading their long blue hair, longer than their bodies all around.

But that near fantasy did not survive for long as Zezi pulled me strong as he found a big trout fish in a cleft nearby. We tried our best but we lost to that crafty and slippery creature. At last, we cheered as it was safe.

While taking a bath, Zezi also collected heaps of fire wood and arranged fire in stones within a minute to prepare rice in a small pan brought in his bag. By keeping the rice on a large leaf he also started preparing 'dal' and boiled beans. He even did not allow me to help him saying that I was his guest on that occasion. He also roasted corn and we then enjoyed cracking corn, while basking, after bath. Then we devoured warm food prepared by Zezi and it was a memorable picnic for me. After that, we came back home sweating heavily and took a bath again.

Blessed is the child who had been taught by his or her parents to enjoy cooking, at least basic food. It is not less than any other educational course to help children grow up as a benign social being and a self-sufficient human.

On the other side of the river 'Zinky', it was Pungro area. It was a long hilly range covered with deep green vegetation. On cloudy days, that area looked mysterious and behind the Pungro range it was a tall feature of Saramati peak, forever enchanting for me. I always wanted to venture in that area up to Saramati. In bright days, some housing or habitation of various villages in Pungro area could be seen clearly from my terrace. The humming sound of loaded Fanta-trucks bringing Fanta from the forest far away on Indo-Myanmer border could be heard. Forest in the area across Pungro range was rich with invaluable teak woods. Some huge and strong rackets were active in that area to befool the local people to cut down and to send huge quantity of log of woods outside every day.

It has always been a discreet soup of discussion in Kiphire that two different sides of 'Zinkyriver' had always been dominated by two different groups of NSCN. There was obviously a periodical change of alienation of the people of two sides of that river to two different currents.

But, nonetheless, to me Pungro area always looked very different and very strange, perhaps for its being nearer to Saramati, I supposed. I met various people from different villages such as Pungro, Salumi, Mimi, Yemikhong, Zanger, Kiusam or Thanamir. I found them very simple but uneasy, a bit uncomfortable and scared in Kiphire town.

30.   The Frightful Night

It was a bitter truth that the underground problem was the most neglected issue on the ground in Nagaland. There was no serious exercise or effort to bring a concrete solution to that problem which caused an untimely end to a number of tender lives. No rational mind could justify those demises.

I can never forget the night when throughout the night there was an operation against NSCN(IM) in Kiphire town itself. It started late in the night, just after dinner, when I was in my bed with some book waiting for sleep to set in my eyes. I heard the sound of a cracker like rattling after being echoed by hills all around. Then after a few moments, it continued for a while. I saw a flush of white light like halogen through the glass of my window. I got up instantaneously from the bed, I smelled something abnormal. I could hear a good number of troupes running on the road with their heavy and hard combat boots. Some of them were shouting to stimulate others. They ran down towards Loyla School on the road in front of my room. I guessed, it was not the sound of crackers but that of firing.

Firing was random by that time. A huge firing was on in between NSCN and Assam Rifles. An illuminating shell of tracer round was fired just a few yards away from my room to the sky, it made the night sky as bright as day for a few seconds. Everything, even every leaf of tree could be seen in that unbelievable light. Under that light, I could guess two-three grenades were thrown on the target area besides showering rapid fires from various automatic weapons. It was incessant firing from both sides. Illuminating bomb and tracer round were being fired by Assam Rifles from various corners sometimes it was from up on the hill near the quarter area of the Superintendent of police, sometimes it was from hospital area and very often it was from the main-junction or market. I was watching those lights in different colours, such as white, orange or yellow from the shell travelling through up in the air carried by little parachutes and hearing thundering sound of firing by standing at my veranda. It was endless. Then there was shouting by the force people. My neighbours started putting out the lights. My neighbouring aunty whispered in a very low voice seeing me in the veranda, "Malik, don't be out of your room. Go inside." At that very moment, I felt something passing very fast whistling just near my left ear. I took some moments to realise what that sound was actually!

I came inside the room at once. She was right. The firing could be from anywhere, anytime. Outside, the firing was just like a heavy rain or shower at that time under the artificial light. A number of parachute bombs were on flight, lofted from various corners of the town, as well as from far away forests and foothills. It was totally a different world except the fact that the sound of firing was horrible. Every shot or every sound would make one shiver and get shocked. Throughout the night, there was firing from both sides from LMG, Carbine, SLR or AK-47. I was thinking about those who might be facing that shower of bullets at that time. It continued ceaselessly till dawn. I could not sleep that night. With the daylight started stepping in on earth all around my room there was sound of heavy combat boots as jawans of Assam Rifles were going back to the camp.

In the morning, we came to know that the Assam Rifles raided a farming area, down below the hydro project site where the NSCN group was staying for that night. Most of the members of that group were inside the thatched farmhouse. It was news of that morning that five NSCN men died and some personnel of Assam Rifles were seriously injured. Late in the morning, people were found running towards the police station. I also went there immediately.

A crowd gathered there in the police station compound. I went near the crowd. All were watching something silently. I peeped into the spot, through gaps among the people in front of me. I was stunned. I saw one body seemingly laid in the pool of blood. I had no idea that red could look so horrible. My sight started going through from the legs of the body. His jungle boots were well tied on his feet, but socks were found wet by blood. Same was the condition of his trouser and shirt. Those were full of blood. There was a thick black good-luck thread tied on his right wrist and that thread struck me. I supposed I knew that good-luck thread. I could not recall specifically where I saw that black good-luck thread?

Black spots of clotted blood were all over his two hands lying on the two sides of his body. His was a juvenile face full of scattered blood clot. The other side of the face was totally torn or smashed by bullet hits. His jaw of that side was completely blown out. Yes, I recognised him. He was Achumong. His nickname was Raja. Very often, he used to come in the afternoon to play cricket with us. He was very polite and a very good wicket keeper and batsman. His physical fitness was outstanding. Catching the ball by diving in the air in his right or left side, as wicket keeper, and then standing just straight on the ground after one or two vaults in the air, just like trained gymnast, was an easy task for him. I never knew from where he used to come! I could not see him anymore. I could not take heart to watch other four dead bodies.

Some of the women were weeping silently. It was an intolerable sight. It was difficult for me to believe that there was any valid reason for such young people to meet their end of life in such a way. It was really a heavy day. It was also very difficult to accept that the dead body of some youths will be kept lying on the soil of open ground in such a poor way for public display.

31.   In Mon District, the Abode of Konyaks

For some special campaign once I went to Mon, the furthermost north-eastern district of Nagaland and stayed there for about ten days. This Konyak tribal dominated district had its interstate border with Assam and Arunachal Pradesh in the north and international boundary with Myanmer in the east. These people used to be master of every sort of battle. They used to be heavy with brutal thrusts on their enemy and at the end of their fighting they used to be back home with the heads of their enemies. Those skulls used to be the proof of their valour and might. Every village used to have a sort of museum, known as 'Morong' for displaying skulls or any other war related memento. These people were also found settled especially in Tirap and Changlang districts of Arunachal Pradesh and in adjacent localities of Myanmar.

To reach Mon by road from Kohima, one had to travel, via Dimapur of Nagaland and Golaghat, Jorhat, Shibsagar town of Assam. It was a long route but the road was very good and so was the side view.

The opening ceremony of that programme was organised at the local stadium at Mon town. Then from Mon we dispersed for various remote villages. Our team, including medical officer and Veterinary officer, was to go towards Myanmer border following Longwa road. But after going for about three hours we reached a place where the wild river had blown away the road following sudden heavy rain in the previous night on the hilltop in Arunachal Pradesh. The river water was so fast and wild that one could not think even to touch that flowing water. We were helpless. So, from that spot, we approached the nearest village Morung. We met the 'Aung', the king of the village. The 'Aung', an elderly man greeted us in his room. He was wearing some typical chain made of stone or bone beads; there were several black tattoos on his forehead, cheeks, nose, ear, chest and arms. And that ever-smiling man had no cloth on his body, but he was at ease. He happily permitted us to carry out our medical and veterinary treatment camp there.

It was a tiny beautiful village. But the sign was everywhere that people were struggling heavily to survive away from any support and aids from the government. There was no health centre, high school or transportation facility available in that area or in the surrounding. They were the real sibling of the soil, from the cradle to the grave, they are sincerely attached and loyal to their native expecting no help or support from any end for their survival and they had proved that they actually did not need any alms or aids. Konyaks were famous being brave warrior. Head hunting was part of their triumph over enemy. They were fearless.

In many houses, skulls were found on display with pride. They were also apt in wooden-craft. The crockery such as plates, spoons, cups, bowls, saucepan, ornaments, toys, other showpieces made of wood were in use in all most all the houses.

In our treatment centre, people came happily to have medical advice or medicines for themselves. Veterinary treatment and medicine distribution centre were also there for their livestock. They were more concerned about their livestock. Most of the elders came at our camp were either in no cloth or with a small loincloth on to cover their waistline. It was a different experience.

We stayed in that village for that night, in the church guest room and in the evening, the Tapan Sinha movie "Safed Hati (White Elephant)" was screened from our projector. All the villagers enjoyed the movie as the vocal language hardly had any significance in the story.

The next morning, we had a programme to proceed to two other villages after having breakfast. We were getting ready for breakfast. At that moment, one of our drivers, a Thangkhul man from Manipur who went for washing the vehicle in the river, came there running with his mouth bleeding heavily. His lips and jaws were found wounded as if he has received some heavy blow of boxing on his jaw. Somehow, he narrated that while he was washing the vehicle in the river water some underground fellow with arms appeared there from the forest and charged him. As he was not so fluent in Nagamese before he could respond to all the queries properly, one of the underground fellows boxed him hard and drove him from the area.

Some villagers at once rushed to the spot and found our vehicle there unhurt. But, none of the underground people was there in the vicinity. At that moment, some of the Gaon-buda revealed that the previous day, at least 5-6 boys from the underground had come in our treatment camp for medicine. The villagers felt so sorry for the incident. The Aung and village elders apologised and assured that such incident will not take place again with any of our team-members.

We had our next camp in a nearby small village in the noon and then we reached the other village on the top of the hill in the evening. There the village head was the Aung. The village authority welcomed us, and we screened the same movie there. All villagers irrespective of age and gender enjoyed a lot. From every corner, the audience's response was coming in with the words 'Yakka', 'Hoi', 'Yamma ma ma' in almost every scene. Kids were very excited as all of them were watching on a big-screen movie for the first time. They were curious to see what was happening in the projector, on the screen or on the backside of the screen.

As we were short of ration, and as there was no shop in that village, we were in need of rice for that night. But to our utter surprise we did not get rice anywhere in the village as all their rice stock for that season had been exhausted and at that time they were solely dependent on corn rice or granules. We got sufficient of that granule. So, we had corn rice, boiled arum, boiled squash and chatni for our dinner that night.

Every family used to keep plenty of granules of corn and small pieces of dried arum, or 'kochu', in big baskets for emergency use as the rice and other vegetables being produced in that area were not sufficient for the whole year for those people. Those two foods were new for others and me. People used to cut 'kochu' into small pieces and get dried in the sun light and stored in huge bamboo-made baskets.

For the villagers seeing the sun every morning and having the privilege to feel the essence or blessings of God was enough to continue living. They were not able to afford adding any more amenities to their daily doings. But poverty or adversity obviously failed to stop those villagers from being happy, honest, helpful and wise.

On that same night, some of our senior officers reached the village to witness the response of people towards our activities. As they could not follow the right track, they were nearly lost on the way and somehow by asking other villagers they reached the village at that late hour. None of the villagers or us was prepared for those guests at that odd hour. They were very hungry so corn rice, arum and chatni were prepared again. They devoured those unique dishes with great pleasure. Then we started gossiping all around the fire in the kitchen of the Aung's house. All were found thrilled to get the opportunity to eat and stay in the house of the Aung. The wooden cots given to us for sleeping were single planks, about 7feet long and about 5 feet wide and those were almost 6 inches thick, a real royal bed. We continued talking till midnight. As in that village we could not manage to get an extra quilt or bedding, the three of us spared our sleeping bags to three elderly seniors. Rest of us again engaged ourselves in gossiping and cracking jokes around the fire rest of the night sipping hot tea time to time.

In the early morning when the time came to be bothered for washroom it was discovered that no well covered latrine or toilet shade was available there. So, the seniors hurriedly apologised to the village elders and the Aung and left the village for Mon town in various important imaginary pretexts.

It was thrilling to sit in the local latrine, under the open sky, on the hill and nearer to nature. It was simply a plank, somehow fixed at the edge of the rocks from where a little flaw can throw one down the steep slope of the hill! One bamboo vertically buried in the ground was of course there for support so that if required the user could hold that. The only cover available there was the small bamboo bush affront, a few metres away. Even then, the user was to sing a song bit loudly so that nobody else would come in that area at that very moment. Moreover, one could see, by looking down, a flock of hungry swine waiting eagerly, grunting with patience, watching upside with their greedy eyes, deep down below on the slope of the hill. They kept on fighting each other for every drop.

32.   Our Office, a Happy Family

We were a happy family in our office, consisting two local Sema boys, one local Sangtam boy, one Chakesang boy from Phek and one elderly man from Bihar, and me. Our office was actually an office-cum-residence. There were differences in habits, in practice or in food-habits but those were not at all larger than our sense of fellow feeling.

Nichiu Chakesang was always happy and was always polite with anybody including strangers. Among Naga boys, he was really far away from his home place. He was from Chojuba under Phek District. He loved chewing 'paan' or tobacco. Almost every evening, he used to drink 'Modhu', local rice beer. He was always ready to help others. He did not know how to save money and he had a peculiar supposition that employees should spend all the monthly salary in full within the respective month. I somehow made him realise that only saving can flourish our future. Then he compelled me to take care of his saving. He started keeping rest of his salary, after paying his dues, with me. Sometimes, in the last week of the month he used beg his money from me, "Sir 'paan' khaboley paisa naai, paisa alop dibo naki. I don't have money to buy 'paan'. Please give me some rupees." Though it was very odd and difficult for me to keep account properly but I tried my best to stand his faith on me. While going on leave for his home I used to hand over all his saving to him and he started enjoying going to his parents with a good amount of money.

If there were no Sema person around, it was generally told among people that Semas were the most short tempered people and not at all negotiable. Most of us were made to feed with such misconception, for sure, on various pretexts in Nagaland. I visited a number of Sema villages in Kiphire and in Zunoboto or Satakha and everywhere I found people to be most courteous, helpful and friendly. While staying at Satakha for some days for some field work, I met one school teacher, in a remote village, who was actually from West Bengal, living in a lovely cottage, at some distance from the village, with his minor son and wife. I was surprised and happy to see them extremely happy there. I spent long hours with that family and I was told by them that they were always being treated with absolute respect by the students as well as by the villagers. Villagers were always truly concerned for their safety, welfare and comfort of the teacher and his family.

Kekheto Sema, the boy in my office was somehow found to have earned a good name for his bad temper. His well-maintained body muscles and tough feature actually compelled people to presume what he was actually not. In one occasion when he was late for some days to report back from leave from the native village I reported the matter to higher headquarters showing him absent from duty. After his coming back, when he was intimated that his absence was reported to headquarters he became so angry and furious that he started shouting and striding hurriedly from one end to another in the office campus. He charged me as how I dared to report the headquarters about his absence. He was shivering in anger. I told him clearly that I could not help him and that what I did was my duty. All of a sudden, he ran fast to a flowerpot of ground orchids and lifted it high in the air and smashed that heavy earthen pot by throwing on the ground in front of me out of rage. I found a sign of relief in his face after he smashed the pot. I took the chance to lift another flowerpot high in the air as Kekheto did and smashed the pot in front of him. Initially he was spellbound and shocked and then he started laughing. I could not guess for what. But I found him to shake off all the ill-sense of anger. I joined him and we laughed for few long minutes. From that day onward, he never committed anything wrong or lost his temper. I found him always very polite.

Besides Lipong, the Sangtam boy was always with me in the field as a guide and assistant. He had better access to all the local villages and good reputation among villagers, which helped me a lot to reach nearer to people. Off and on, I got assistance of some staff members who hailed from Assam, Bihar, U.P. or Tripura who had been posted for a small duration in Kiphire.

I enjoyed working in other places also as and when entrusted with any specific task. I was in Wokha for few days. That headquarter of Wokha district, bordering with Assam and it was home to the Lotha people. I visited

Tsemenyu area many times to work with Rengma people. These ever-smiling people were extremely laborious. I got benign company of Rengma youths for working in the villages around Tsemenyu area. I was privileged to visit and stay in various Rengma villages such as Tseminyu, Kasanyu, Nsunyu, Zisunyu or Sendenyu under Kohima district.

Lotha and Rengma boys, who had been in Kiphire with me for some time, were also found very intelligent and sociable to adopt effectively to work in the field in faraway villages of Sangtam, Sema or Yimchuger people.

Our office was a common destination for people of all the remote villages of Kiphire Sub-division as they used to come to our office whenever they came to Kiphire for any work or any issue. They talked to me on all prevailing issues or problem pertaining to their locality. They were welcome to take rest at our office campus after their long treks to reach Kiphire from their village. So, we had a cordial cord with all those people transcending their racial identity.

Very often villagers used to say, "Paisa to 'Laipatta' achhey de, sir, aani thakibo aroo khai kina khatam kori thakibo! Aaroo amakhan relation ekdom prithbi khatam hoa tok thakibo de. Hoi na nahoi? (Sir, money is just like 'Laipatta' or green leaves, it is brought and it gets exhausted. But our relation keeps us connected forever. Is not it?)" So every moment in Nagaland, I appeared to be learning all small and important ethics of living or life.

33. Sweet Memory of Moya

'Moya' a remote village in Pungro area always had, and still has, a special corner in my heart. It was nearer to Myanmer border and nearer to Saramati peak. It was one of the very few villages located not on the hilltop but at the foothill or low land surrounded by forest and high hill in all directions. So, it was a bit hot in summer. The chairman of the village, Kiusimong was a good friend of mine. He was young, active and friendly. He took much pain for betterment of that one of the remotest village and its villagers. We met in the ADC office at Kiphire for the first time out of occasion and as I was good at listening, we became friends. He used to come to Kiphire frequently and whenever he was there at Kiphire he used to come to our office.

One day he came to me and said, "Malik, I have managed to get some sticks of gelatine. I know you like fish. So come with me to my village. We will have an outing for fishing in the spring and river there and have grand picnic! Amakhan jangaltey nodi pora machh dhoribo aaroo moja pora picnic karibo. Please don't say no."

He showed me five gelatine sticks he managed from the GREF people.

But as I had some immediate work at that time I was not in position to leave for Moya on that very day. I requested him to allow me some time so that I could complete the work and come to their village.

So I said, "Dui teen din bhitorte ahiboi… ahibo! I will definitely come there within two or three days. I promise! Kassam!" I did swear by biting my right index finger, in Naga style.

Once I had visited that village for a while. I remembered that a few months back, I had reached the village with some construction materials for a little project for the village. On that occasion, we were three, Lipong, driver Iyanger and me. I was sitting at a window of the one-toner truck loaded with cement, rods and bricks, while Lipong was sitting in between the driver and me. The road was horrible and so we crossed or came across no other vehicle other than one or two 'Fanta-trucks'. It was the first time for me to cross 'Zinky' river and to enter into Pungro. After crossing Pungro town, we were on the narrow road through a deep jungle.

Pungro was rich of bright greenness and was splendidly beautiful. In my side, it was flora on the steep high hill and on the other hand, in driver's side, it was deep and dark ravine across a few feet of jungle rich of bamboo trees and wild bushes. Our vehicle was moving very slowly on 2nd or 1st gear on that muddy and narrow road. Even then, we enjoyed the journey by watching the beautiful greenery. All of a sudden, two armed men in combat dress jumped at both the windows from both sides of the road and before I could appreciate anything, the cruel cold barrel of AK-47 of that man was placed on my throat harshly. It was pressing my throat painfully. The other guy did the same thing with the driver Iyanger. The vehicle was stopped.

That man started questioning me. I replied all his queries with that barrel still sitting harshly on my throat. As I was talking to him, and Lipong tried to convince them, the barrel was getting away gradually from my throat. I was sweating heavily. For me it was hard to believe that I was not shot or nothing penetrated through my throat. I was actually praying to Almighty God.

They enquired about our reason for our going towards Moya, about our work and activities. Finally, they apologised for everything. They stated that as soldiers of NSCN(K) it was their duty to check all undue movements on that road as they were deployed there for that purpose. So Pungro area was being dominated by NSCN(K) at that period of time. Iyanger was so scared. He was actually shocked, a shocked me guessed. He could not utter a word. Lipong talked to them in Sangtam language. We were told to avoid any movement after sunset. So that day, we reached Moya at about 1130 am and after dropping those goods we left the village at about 0200 pm and reached at Kiphire at about 0800 pm. Iyanger regained himself after reaching Kiphire. He started talking freely. So it was a brief, very brief visit to Moya due to a bad situation and as emphasised by locals to avoid staying there.

So, I decided to go to Moya that time as I was invited for fishing and picnic. We tied up the programme to reach Moya with one of my friend from Pungro who was going back there with his jeep from Kiphire. Though he insisted that he will send his vehicle up to Moya but I ensured him not to be worried as I would enjoy walking, moreover the road was not good for the vehicle.

After two days, we, Lipong and me, came up to Pungro by that jeep with that friend. Pungro a small town on a valley type land on the top of the hill was vibrant with green and it allowed all to have a bright view of the Saramati peak. We had lunch at the house of my friend. Then we started from Pungro at about 11 am for Moya following state road. No vehicles except one or two GREF trucks were found on that road. Except that road, everything was rightly in place to enchant us. Hills, forest, streams, rivulets, blue sky, smiling locals and many other still or moving things were there to render nobody the least chance to be in the gloomy. We enjoyed walking by meeting and talking to the villagers of surrounding villages, especially in the road junctions. We got a teashop in a junction near one GREF post and had hot tea there. In one roadside village, we again took rest for a while. Time was running too fast so we took stride steps and following that road we reached the junction where approach road for Moya village was on its own direction downwards.

It was already past evening. It was our turn to walk downwards through the forest along the even slope. Finally at about 8 pm, we reached in front of the huge gate of the village, which was closed from inside. I said gate. Yes, it was a huge and tall gate made of wood and bamboo! In fact, that village was fenced all around by high wall made of woods, bamboos and canes. The wall was 8-9 ft high and about 2 ft wide. As told by Lipong, we stopped a few yards away from the gate helplessly. He said that when the gate was closed then there must be someone or many as guards at or near the gate. There was a watchtower indeed just on the other side of the fence but that was found not manned at that point of time. After a while, Lipong shouted in Sangtam and in Yimchunger language in the direction of the village. It was cold, it was dark and it was a state of absolute silence, except some crickets making noises from a distance.

He shouted again keeping his palms in front of his mouth like a microphone, "Is anybody there? We are guests from Kiphire, waiting here. Can anybody hear me?"

There was some sound of somebody coming fast. There was some movement on the watchtower and then the focus of torch light caught us. The man enquired about us from Lipong by shouting from the tower. Then he again rushed to the village excitingly, leaving us in the dark. And after about a long 10 minutes Kiusimong, the village chairman along with five others, came at the gate and from the tiny window of the gate he flashed his light on us and shouted, "Oh! Sorry, sorry, sorry, Malik sir, so sorry. Ahibi, ahibi. Hochha ahi se de sir. Beshi khusi paise de. You have really reached here. So happy we are! Ekta khabar dibo lagichhile. We should have been informed earlier. Besi digdar paichhey hola. Motor cycle ekta pathai dibo thakichhile. You suffered a lot. I could have sent some motorcycles." The gate was opened at once with a typical shrilling sound, the chairman took us inside, and the heavy gate was closed again by setting two or three long wooden posts.

I knew such fencing or wall was part of security measure adopted by the Naga villages, since long, long back, to protect their people and other assets from any sort of attack by the intruders. However, Moya village was one of the very few villages in Nagaland that was still using such walls and gate systems as a daily practice. The chairman briefed us that the wall was there in between them and their enemy since time immemorial. He also said that such wall was still significant for their village being located in a low land and near to the perennial stream, where there was frequent movement of wild deer, cows, goats, etc. for drinking water and movement of leopards, tigers, bears, jackals etc in search of those thirsty preys, as well as, for drinking water. Hence, there was every chance that those wild carnivorous would venture into the village and intrude the stable of their livestock. Even the smaller creatures like cats or squirrel could not cross that wall. Many a times, corpses of those animals were found perforated by the sharp-headed spears made of bamboos, set in that wall dangerously.

So, till that time, after the gate was closed in the evening, no unwanted person would be allowed to enter into the village. However, I saw such a wall in many other villages in every part of Nagaland but I never experienced or felt the near-incorrigible presence of such a wall in practicality.

Then I had a sound sleep after a nice dinner, which was freshly prepared by Mrs. Kiusimong in that late hour. We got up early the next morning and found the chairman busy arranging all about the proposed fishing. Within an hour we along with a huge group, especially of youths and kids set off for the stream for fishing and picnic.

Youths and kids were singing, gossiping and laughing loudly while walking through the forest towards the stream or river which was around three kilometres away from the village. Within a few minutes, we reached the place. It was as beautiful as a Christmas card. It was an open area on a mild spur, almost like a huge green golf-ground in the patch of green forest surrounded by the sky touching hills in all directions. To add more beauty, there was a not-so-small-stream after water of some one or more rivulets diving down from high hilly rock, just like a waterfall, touched the rocky ground with heavy thrust creating a small lake of clean and blue water. Stream-water was flying a bit by bouncing off from falling on the rock, creating a fountain of splashing water and mist, from where a beautiful river was originated. It was really a scenic beauty and deserved to be considered as a tourist place. A few yards away on the other side of the river, there was a GREF camp, inhabited by labours from Santhal, Munda communities hired from Orisha, Bihar or West Bengal.

All were getting ready for fishing preparing havoc to fix gelatine, detonator and igniters perfectly on a small boulder with ropes so that when thrown, the boulder would reach deep in to the water with the charge. I, in all possible way, tried to look calm and to reflect no excitement in my appearance, as I had never ever experienced such fishing even in my dream. Some experts were busy preparing round-shaped nets at the top of the bamboos, as usually done to catch a butterfly, to pick up fishes from water by standing at the sides of the lake, the moment fishes came out upwards from the depth after the blast. The lake was not so deep. The water level was hardly up to the chest or throat of a normal adult, I guessed. So clear was the water that we could even see clearly the sand, pebbles or all other creatures under water!

Then after a while, following a cautionary howl to everybody in the surrounding the first charge of gelatine was thrown in the middle of the lake. The detonator was aptly set and ignited hence the boulder went straight in to the deep, creating lots of bubbles rushing upwards, and after a fraction of a second there was a huge blast with rocking sound and flush of water rocketing straight towards the sky like white shell. Silver coloured sand came out in a rush from the deep along with spinning water. Some pebbles or splinters of boulder also came out like bullets from the deep by piercing water. It was awesome. It was thrilling. After free flying in the open for a while, the large and small drops of water came back to the lake again with tinkling sound like heavy drops of rain.

The silence following the blast (which made all birds or animals baffled and silent out of fear of uncertainty) ended as some of the living beings dared to discover that they were alive by tweeting, and all of a sudden, most of the birds and some animals, especially cows and dogs, joined the chorus to claim their lively presence. By the time, the echo of the thundering sound created by the hills in all directions also ended after getting tired and exhausted. The whirling of water also became normal except a few huge bubbles were still coming out from the centre of the blast at the bottom of the lake with typical sound "Zaa … Za … Za … Zaa … Za…"

Then the real magic started. A huge number of small fishes, and some big ones with glittering silver-white bodies started coming up along with those bubbles. It was like a continuous rotation of numerous fishes in the water in cyclic motion. For us, that unending flow of fishes looked like numerous glittering and sparkling particles in that blue water. There was a huge hue and cheers in joy and excitement among villagers. After the initial excitement, people started picking up fishes with the help of those nets. Every sinking net was coming out from the water with plenty of fishes.

I found some big fishes seemingly in an inebriated condition left their body to float abruptly. It was wonderful. A good number of small fishes were found floating towards the flow of water along the river and small kids started catching fishes by hand in that knee-deep river water. As none of the villagers knew swimming, none plunged in to the water to enjoy catching those helpless fishes; instead, they remained busy in netting. I was not a bad swimmer so I could not resist myself from having a strong desire to go deep in to that water and chase those crazy fishes.

My longing got better of me and I decided to explore the lake-water. I undid myself to my shorts and dived in to the hurl of fishes. The chilling cold water hugged my body to the core with its icy smack. It became very refreshing after a while. I took a long breath and went deep up to the bottom of the lake. It was crystal clear there and I could see all the lines in my palm or all my ducts. I was able to see everything around me, from tiny pebbles to all living beings. Fishes were in semi-unconscious condition due to the vibration caused by the blast, those were not even aware of my presence in their sphere. They were rubbing their body with that of mine. I caught one or two huge trout there and then freed them to let them go and I caught them again.

It was just a fantasy that most of us could have only in our dream, and for me it was really like a dream. I had never ever imagined having the opportunity to see or touch fishes in that way. Then I came out exploring the water with two huge fishes in my two hands and threw those in to the crowd. There was huge clap, cheers and roar. I again went under water and came out with two more fishes and threw those in to the air. By that time, I found Lipong and some of the boys were already in waist deep water and were catching fishes with great enthusiasm. It was an inexpressible joy. Once Lipong jumped out of water with three big fishes, two in hands and third one in his mouth and after throwing those in the crowd he was smiling proudly displaying all his teeth. We then came out of the water.

I really forgot that I was in public in my shorts only and all were enjoying watching me swimming in the lake. The kid in me dared to motivate me to forget everything else. After a while, the second charge was lofted into the water. I again dived in search of fishes and there were so many to volunteer to follow me to catch fishes. We caught a huge heap of coruscating fishes and those were enough to be relished by all the villagers so we dropped the idea for any more use of gelatine that occasion.

By that time, boys already gathered a pile of dry firewood and ladies also started cooking by making oven by boulders on that river side. After taking an unforgettable bath in cold water I enjoyed basking in that golden sunlight with hot tea. In the meantime, the rest of the villagers reached there and we witnessed a traditional dance and singing by the young as well as elders. It was a gala gathering of happy hearts there.

We reached the final phase of the picnic, we gathered all around the fresh dishes of food. Some big bowls were filled up with boiled Laipatta, squash, beans and cabbage. One such bowl was full of fish-curry, which was actually fish boiled with Naga-chilly, local tomato, salt and no oil or spices. Rice and varieties of chutney made of various local herbs, roasted fish, soya bean and Naga-chilly had been displayed on banana leaves on the ground. We all prayed to God for happiness of everyone and then we started taking food in a plate from those bowls. It was a grand picnic, it was surfeiting.

I must admit that it was never ever even in my imagination that such a delicious fish curry could be prepared without using spices or oil. I learnt that oil or spices should never be used for cooking fresh fishes, those actually hijack the real taste of fish. That jamboree actually did not conclude at the picnic spot itself. Boys and girls continued singing by playing guitars until we reached the village in the retiring light of sundown making the top of the Saramati peak reddish. I wished I were there on the peak of the Saramati someday to see the sunset from there.

34.   Golden Dream and the Saramati Peak

By the time we reached the valley on the lap of the Saramati peak it was noon, it was very hot; it was prickly as all our dresses were wet with salty sweat. It was only about 500-600 feet down beneath the top of the peak. Our team, consisting of Lipong, Kiusimong, the Chairman of Moya village, and me, decided to take rest for long while before starting further mountaineering to reach the peak. We took rest previous night at Thanamir village, the last hamlet before reaching the Saramati from the Indian side. We started walking early in the morning from Thanamir village. The peak was just on the border of India and Burma (Myanmar).

The small and arid dell was mostly covered with large and small rocks, white and yellow in colour. Many thickets of thorny herbs were also scattered here and there. A few large tamarisk and berry trees were only there to protect one from the heat of the sun. Rest of the ground was found covered with pebbles and sandy soil. So we took shelter under the shadow of a huge berry tree and allowed our body to have some recess. There were a group of argala or cranes a few metres away on another berry bush seemingly annoyed for our presence there. There were some big and small caves or gorges in that rocky vicinity. As a whole, the peak and the area were looking so mysterious and strange that I would not be least surprised if one or more dinosaurs or other prehistoric monsters would come out from those caves. Somehow, for me it was thrilling. I was apparently waiting for those dinosaurs to come out.

We were lucky a cool breeze reached there soon and hugged us. It was a great relief and soon we shook off all the sense of fatigue. It was the clear blue sky greeting me whenever I was opening my eyes by lying there on my back. I pulled my body up and sat down at ease and discovered the unending undulating valley covered with green just down below, looked like a green canyon with some dark or black patch. I could see Kiphire town from there. I could not believe that I was there and I could have nearly a bird's eye view of the southeastern part of Nagaland as well as a vast area of Manipur.

All of a sudden, I realised there was a certain change in the agility of those argala and brisk movement among some other unknown birds, who flew out of the bushes nearby and started crying, seemingly out of panic. I could guess there was some sound of hoofs of horses on the run at a distance and those were nearing towards us. The sound came very near and we saw an eruption of huge dust from just behind the rock in front of us a few metres away. Kiusimong jumped and managed to lead us to hide in thundering speed behind a bush in a small gorge. I could watch from that bush that a group of about 15 men in loose fitting black jubbah-like dress and their faces were covered with deep black cloth. They had huge turbans of silky cloth with black and white stripes like a chessboard.

Their well-built body and tough body language beckoned that they must be very dangerous and ruthless plunderers. All those yellowish-white skinned men were on tall and stout horses. On their back, there was a spear fitted on a metalled shield and almost all of them were holding heavy swords. The man who looked like their leader was having a single barrel old-model gun. They were on the other side of the curtain of huge dust. Those horses were breathing heavily and rubbing their hoofs restlessly on the soil. The area became full of some horrible wild fetid smell. Lipong almost fainted. I was watching them insensitively and Kiusimong seemed to have some courage and sense left to tell us to breathe silently and pray to God.

The leader of that group was passing various instructions to the group members in some unknown and unintelligible language. Only he was talking and others were listening to him like statues. Then after a while, they all jumped down from horseback and gathered in front of the big berry bush under the steep rock and keeping only two persons and all their horses, standing there, all disappeared in that thorny bush within a moment.

We were also doing our best to carry out the most difficult work, befitting such an occasion, and it was to keep ourselves speechless and motionless. All of a sudden, the group came out of the bush and discussed among themselves for some moment there and then they got seated on the horseback like springs and with their hill to kick at the lower abdomen of those well-trained horses they rushed out of our sight within a few second.

We were sweating a lot but Kiusimong told us not to move or raise our head for some minutes. After a long pause, Kiusimong started crawling to get out of the gorge and went out and he then whispered towards us to come out. We came out in the open and found ourselves breathing in a normal pace and pitch. I wanted to tell you something about that very berry bush where the group was found to get disappeared and Kiusimong understood. So we enter into that bush, it was thorny and we got so many painful scratches in our hands, chests and face. As we went forward a few steps, there appeared the opening of a cave and impressions of huge shoes of those people beckoned that they went inside that dark cave.

All three of us were in the opinion to leave the place immediately but after having a look in to the cave, we decided to face all eventualities together and stepped in towards the dark opening of that cave. It was so dark inside the cave that nothing could be seen neither there was any sound. Kiusimong was leading us and I found his eyes glittering and sparking in that mysterious dark. My left hand was in the tight grip of that of Kiusimong's and behind me, it was Lipong. After a while, we found our eyes started working. Our eyesight could guess things well by piercing the curtain of darkness. We could hear mild tinkling of thin stream inside. We were able to distinguish the wall of the cave, the boulders, the hole or mud or thin drain of water under our feet. In some places, the wet and rocky wall of the cave was so cold that I shivered heavily thinking of the body of huge reptiles.

Ruthless Arakan tyrant

After a few steps we found some cold breeze coming from the inner side, and though we knew that we came far inside the cave and going back was the best option before us but it seemed as if we had been hypnotised by some unknown spirit and there was no returning back. We reached bit wide flat space and realised that our surrounding was not dark but a strange yellowish radiation coming from all most every corner of the wall of that huge hall type space.

We realised all wall was golden yellow, the soil was golden yellow and in a corner a huge boulder was glittering a bit with dim-yellow light from inside as if it was made of gold. I looked upside and saw the roof was also yellowish. Many tall conical yellowish column with sharpen edge facing the ground were found hanging from the roof. Those columns looked wet or oily. Wall was not smooth but looked like some uneven cluster of beehive. And to our utter surprise everything there seemed to be made of gold, no I was wrong, actually nothing but gold was heaped there.

"Oh! My God." I almost broke down.

Lipongba started mumbling from Holy Bible praying to God to come to our rescue, as if we had been trapped by gold. Kiusimong was speechless. He walked towards that mound of gold and extended his right hand to touch the mound. A sudden spark from the hand of Kiusimong dazed our eyes and to our utter surprise, we saw the thick iron bangle in his wrist turned gold. Oh! God. It must be the so-called 'philosopher's stone'. I gulped. I was extremely frightened and nervous. All of a sudden, we realised the movement of some living being in the wall opposite to us. It appeared as if whole wall was inhaling and exhaling with mild tremble all over the wall. We saw a massive serpent, just behind that magic-mound, seemingly breaking hibernation and dislodging coil of its body. It was a giant snake. It was yawning by throwing its huge bisected teeth or tongue ruthlessly. The queer sound from the body of the serpent gradually moving this side or that side made me motionless. Though I remembered that somewhere I heard or read that we must not look straight to the eyes of any serpent as they have the ability to hypnotise, I already lost all my physical strength.

I could remember Kiusimong pulled me strongly towards the opening of the cave and shouted "Malik, run. Run fast."

I got my sense back. We ran fast. Kiusimong kept on holding my hand. Lipong was ahead of us. I only knew that the huge snake was coming fast behind us with its spiral way by getting scaled body with the wall of the cave causing a horrified sound. We could hear the sound of many other reptiles, insects, wild animals behind us. A huge group of bats or titmouse crossed us fast, flying with a shrilling scream, to get out of the cave and vanished in the firmament. We could see the opening of the cave in our sight and we could see the bush outside from there. Lipong was already out of the cave. And soon we threw our body out of the cave.

Kiusimong and me came out of the bush and fell down on the ground. It was dust all-round and I was in need of at least some drops of drinking water. My throat was so dry that I could not even spit. But lying on the ground I heard the sound of hoofs. I raised my head a bit and saw almost unconsciously that Kiusimong and I were lying on the dust surrounded by horses and on the back of those horses, there were those Arakans or Mogs or Hun staring at us with cruel and angry eyes. Those horses were knocking their hoofs on the sandy-ground abruptly making all around covered in dust. I knew our end had come. I wanted to see the sky, so I stared to the sky and saw one of those plunderer to hold Lipong by his collar by sitting on the horseback by one hand placing his heavy sword just on Lipong's throat by the other hand. Lipong's body was hanging from the fist of that demon. I cried, "Please, leave him. Leave him please."

Another pair of hands touched my throat and collar to lift me in the air. The grip on my collar was so tight that I could not breathe at all. I was choking. I was in need of air and a few drops of water. My eyes started erupting out of the sockets due to want of breath. I could see the black, deep black smoke of death coming fast towards me. I threw my hands with all my strength for the last time. The man left my collar and threw my body straight on the ground. I groaned in pain. Kiusimong crawled to me and shouted, "Sir, Sir, Malik."

"Sir, sir, Malik Malik." Yes it was Kiusimong's voice. "Good Morning. Let us have tea. It is too late."

I got up by jumping like a spring. I was baffled. It was Kiusimong indeed. So, I was in the land of nod. It was a dream! I was exhausted; I was dried with thirst, I drank a lot of water. But I was so happy that we were alive. I was sleeping in the guest room of the chairman, and was suffering from a ruthless dream, a real nightmare.

It was sunny outside. And there Lipong was talking loudly in a jolly mood with some of the villagers. I was so relieved. I stared to the right wrist of Kiusimong and the thick iron bangle was gracing the wrist.

I came out of the room with tea and looked towards the Saramati. It was shining by smearing radiance of the morning sun. I found the peak bantering. But there was fable about the Saramati was rich of gold-mine. May be I was almost in that mine. However, I will never forget that journey of mine, in my dream, to the Saramati, the time I spent on it. It might be in my dream, but I did not care. I was back to real life with lot, lot of gold in my mind. I wish that gold of hope I got from the Saramati would be endless.

35.　　　　　　　Me on Gunpoint

That morning was quite different; every corner of the town was covered by dense fog and mist. It was chilling cold. I was not in mood to leave the warm lap of my quilt but as I was to proceed for Meluri by local bus, I got ready by 5:30 am. Outside it was almost drizzling. Such a cool and wet morning came seldom in my life in Nagaland. But, that very morning was of different nature for the cold was accompanied with fog, mist, rain and Kiphire looked invaded by the cloud. Intension of the nature was very clear since dawn that we were going to have a day without sunshine in Kiphire. Even the cock-a-doodle-doo by the rooster all around the town in the dawn failed to appease the sun to peep in with a single beam.

I could not see anything away from me by a few feet. I was wearing a heavy jacket on a full sweater on the full sleeve shirt on a thick inner to protect me from the body piercing cold with a muffler covering my neck, ear and head. I kept one Sangtam shawl also on my soldier in a ready condition to wrap me after I board in to the bus. All at the bus stand were found in their heaviest outfit either rubbing their right palm with the left one or left one with the right palm while ejecting huge vapour with their every breathe.

There was no NST, i.e. Nagaland State Transport, bus service that day. So the private mini bus was the only option for us to move towards Kohima. Fortunately, I got one ticket. The bus driver, a young chap, namely Shelongpa, was blowing the horn repeatedly to bring some more passengers to get in to the bus. At that moment one Assam Rifle bus full of local people appearing to be a cultural troupe with a lot of hue and cheers and choir passed through that area before us.

It was the Sangtam traditional dance troupe of Kiphire village going to Kohima to perform in the Naga-festival in Army Headquarters at Zakhama in Kohima. Assam Rifle provided the bus for the transportation of the troupe. So the troupe assembled in the Assam Rifle camp early in the morning to reach Kohima in time.

After a few minutes, our bus left the bus stand full of passengers and on the way it kept on picking up local passengers until it did cross the Kiphire village bus stop. After crossing Kiphire village our bus picked up well and going down along the spiral road on the hilly slope with a good speed though visibility was very poor due to heavy fog, as if we were moving by piercing endless cloud.

In clear weather, while travelling by bus one can enjoy watching the well-groomed and decorated cultivated land or green vegetation in the hilly slope and then the Blue Zinky river deep down the hill. However, we were proceeding ahead by listening gospel as was being sung by two-three ladies in the rear. The more we were going away from Kiphire hill the more we were away from the fog. Weather was nearly clear in that area.

After covering about 20 kilometres we reached near dense forest area down below Sanphure village and found the same Assam Rifle bus was standing, a few metres ahead of us, on the mid of the road among crowd. We presumed that the vehicle might have met with some defects with engine or tyre. Some of the passengers got down from the bus to roam around. I tried to close my eyes to have a short rest for eyesight. But within a few second we came to know that the Assam Rifles bus was stopped by a group of NSCN(IM). The group was seemingly very angry and furious as the villagers of Kiphire village were going to take part in the programme of Indian Army defying the ultimatum of NSCN(IM) that locals not to take part in any occasion of Indian Army. The group made all the villagers come out from that Assam Rifles bus and stand in a line on the road. I found that every face in our bus had become pale in fear. All the passengers got in to the bus at once.

Within a few moments, the commander of the group came along with two more cadres, all armed with sophisticated weapons, near our bus. The commander came inside the bus and stared at all the passengers with angry eyes. He ordered all Indians or non-Nagas to get down from the bus. At that very moment, I discovered all the passengers turn their eyes towards me, as I was the only non-Naga face there in that bus. I got down from the bus. Two NSCN boys held my arms tightly and pushed me forward towards the Assam Rifle bus. I found the area well cordoned by the cadres. Every patch of forest or ridge of the hillock was being guarded by NSCN cadres, mostly young boys, armed with AK-47, SLR, carbines or LMG. Some of them had a chain of grenades on their waist. My throat dried up.

I was taken to the front side of the bus. There I found that three Assam Rifles personnel, the driver and two others (who were escorting the dance troupe and the vehicle) had been made to be on their knees. Their hands were tied at their back. They were also blindfolded by tying their eyes with handkerchief or towel. I found a huge roll of cortex; soaps and charges of explosives were dumped in front of that bus. On the same line and with those poor Assam Rifles personnel I was also made to kneel down. My hands were tied tightly at my back. My eyes were also tied with a stingy black cloth.

The angry commander of that group was shouting in Sangtam language as well as in Nagamese that he will kill all four of us, and set the Assam Rifle bus on fire by explosion for the sins on the part of those villagers of Kiphire. The villagers started shouting for mercy and for our life. Women started crying and weeping. I could hear male members led by the Personal Assistant to the ADC of Kiphire, who was also the gaon-bura of the Kiphire village, come forward and apologise to the commander, praying for mercy, and begging for our life. I could recognise his voice.

I started counting every second and began praying to the God if He could come to our rescue, or otherwise to forgive me for my misdeeds, if there were any. I was not in the state to think straight or properly but an inevitable strong thrust of weeping continued to precipitate from the deepest of my heart for my kin, my friends, for everything under the sky and those beyond the space as I realised that at any moment I could meet the fatal consequence.

All of a sudden, I heard a harsh shout by the commander ordering the boys to fire, and within a moment I was among the thundering sound of huge rapid-fire all around me. I guessed some the shots passed just kissing my ears or skull. They fired in the air at random to threaten and to make the villagers disperse and to leave the place. The sound of the crowd running away from that area faded gradually in my sense, as the crowd left that place at once out of fear, before the echo of those rumbling shots from the hills had been exhausted. There remained only those rebels, deaf nature and of course, our remorse filled bodies and our silently weeping soul.

I was blown heavily on my shoulder with the butt of an arm and forced to get up and walk. My arm was held tightly and I was being dragged by collar towards another place up the hill. I guessed we were being taken too deep into the forest, up on the hill. My face and dress got so many scrapes. I could not remember how many times I was knocked by the butt or barrel on my chest, back and belly, and I still shiver up and down the spine remembering the stifling smell of those barrels bruising my ears or head or cheeks to force me to walk fast. Even the freezing mercury failed to resist me from sweating profusely. We walked for quite a long time and then I was thrown to the ground to lie down on my chest. Even the birds in that forest did not dare to make any sound. I guessed three other captives were kept in separate places in that vicinity. I could hear one of the Assam Rifles men, might be from South India, screaming as he was being beaten heavily for his not being able to talk in Nagamese in the course of interrogation. I knew it would my turn after a few minutes.

One of those custodians came to me and pulled me up to sit down. I was slapped and knocked heavily by strong fists and arms, I supposed without valid reason, just to introduce me with the nature and consequence of that interrogation phase. My soul wept in pain. I was proud to be fluent in Nagamese and so, as I believed, I was able to appease them with my response to their queries. They also checked my pockets, purse and identity card.

By the grace of God, I was again made to lie down on my chest and left alone, I guessed, for long to make me endure the torment. All my clothing were already wet by sweating, then there was pain in every part of my body, the sense of itching all over my face, thirst in each and every cell, and more over my hands at my back were also arrested by rigorous knots and my sight was in absolute darkness as my eyes were made to cease seeing. And all these facts showered an inexpressible congregation of pain and anguish upon me. Every moment seemed as long as years.

I was eager to hear the sound of water being poured in a glass and to have somebody to offer me at least a few drops of water. I started thinking thorough whether I had done anything wrong or was I wrong to opt to work there. But from no end of my conscience I got any instance of wrong on the part of any of the locals or on that of mine which might have caused such ill-fated moments for me. I have always been keen to do justice with my present so that I do not indulge in committing anything wrong at any moment. I have seen many present become the past, many futures to turn into the present and then merge with the past. There was no answer for questions such as why we were or I was suffering in that way. I shared all the torments within my flesh and within my soul with the mother-earth, as it was the closest body to my body at that moment. I told the earth all the sweet and all the bitter tales of my life. My mind was venturing all the lanes of my native to see all my kin and my friends, the school, college, the pool or the playground. I cannot remember what else I was thinking about. Lastly, I seemed I was in the opinion as if I were not born till that time. I was yet to be born. I was almost going through a state of lunacy; it was swinging beyond time and space. I did not know whether that spiritless corpse of mine was actually sleeping or otherwise.

I did not know after how many hours I was knocked again. I felt some mild knock on my back. I guessed some people were coming to that place. I forgot to respond. I should have wept, I should have begged for my life. But I miserably lost all my sense. Some hands pulled me up to make me stand and then I was again dragged a few metres downwards. The world was still deep dark for me. I could hear a gathering discussing. I got a friendly touch of hand on my cheek and on my shoulder. Some soft words reached all my cells "Malik, ... sir," those hands untied all knots on my head and my hands. I was not able to open my eyes. I was not in position to stand. Those men shook me and held me tight. I managed to open my eyes and after struggling a lot in facing the shining of daylight, to my utter surprise, I found the Chairman of Sanphure village Mr. Khamong in front of me. He was there, along with a group of the gaon-buras in their traditional attire. They greeted me and the subconscious mind in me discovered the God, the saviour, in those villagers.

I almost fainted. I miserably failed to gather strength in my knees or legs. I sat down on the ground. I found myself among the Chairman and Gaon-buras of Sanphure village, cordoned by those NSCN men. I got my breath back. The commander of that group came near me hold my hand in his fist and apologised, "Sorry. Sorry for all that faced by you. Bye." "It's okay," I said by using my eyes, I supposed. Then with the help of those villagers, for my every step downwards, I slowly came down to the road again. It was deserted. But the Assam Rifle bus was still there.

We sat at the roadside. Mr. Khamong apologised for the trouble. He briefed me that it was a very close save for me. He said that in the morning they heard the sound of huge firing from that area on the road, just about two kilometres from their village, down below the hill. While going down to the farm for cultivation one of the villagers, from behind the bush or jungle, found some movement of those armed persons in the area where we, the captives, were being interrogated. It was absolutely fortunate for me that the man could recognise me and without wasting any time, that man went back to the village running all the steep-height and reported the matter to the Chairman Mr. Khamong.

Appreciating the situation, Mr. Khamong along with gaon-buras and some youths, straightaway came down to the spot, putting traditional dress on and met the Commander of the NSCN group. They requested the commander to cause no harm to me. In Nagaland, till that time the village body, of Chairman and gaon-buras, in their traditional attire were supremely empowered within the respective area. As the area was under the territory of Sanphure village council, the commander, following a long discussion, gave all respect to the urge of the villagers and set me free.

I got my life back only for the wisdom and timely intervention by those villagers. They rushed down to save me because they knew me well. I stayed with them in their village for somedays. I had been able to have some youths, as our volunteers, to assist us in field. I owed my blessed ambit to resume living to the villagers of Sanphure.

I was again surprised seeing that Shelongpa, the driver of the minibus, by which I was travelling that very morning, coming from a few distance behind with the vehicle. The driver, the boy from Kiphire was waiting whole day for me with hope that I would come back safe. He did not leave the place though all the passengers went back to Kiphire on foot. So I was fortunate enough to be among those real good Samaritans. Mr. Khamong and all the gaon-buras helped me to sit in the bus and prayed for my long life. Then we parted for the time being.

No other passenger was there in the bus. That great driver waited there only for me. He drove fast and at about 8 pm we reached at Meluri. He helped me to get down from the bus, to enter into the room and to lie down on the bed. I was in a state of obsession; I could not get myself out of that nightmare. It was very difficult for me to believe that I was alive.

We stayed in our office in Meluri for the night. Early in the morning, that driver left Meluri for Kohima. After long sound sleep that night, I could start recuperating to pray to God. I was really obliged to Him for considering me to live more. I thanked Him for sending those Naga friends of Sanphure in that decisive moment. However, after a few days I came back to Kiphire and started working again. I was happy to be back again at Kiphire. It was also great to hear that those Assam Rifles Jawans were also released by the NSCN after two or three days.

So the facts behind attuning that blissful vivification of mine, before my eyes, was not merely telling tales, it was, as I believed, due to hard earned attachment with the villagers and blessing of the Almighty who seemed wanted me to do better.

36.

Atila, the Knight

A tila was a close friend of mine. She was the eldest among two daughters of Mr. Atoshie. Atila and her sister Atsi never needed any care or formalities to invade my room or to lead conversation with me. The lean and thin feature of Atila was very near to a true zero figure. She shaped her golden hair in a boyish-style. She seemingly used to wake up in the morning to talk on any topic and to keep on talking till her going to bed again at night. On the other hand Atsi was a bit fat and had long black hair. She was friendly but a bit reserved and always used to be in apt make up with deep red lipstick.

Atila was working in a State Govt. Office, and used to go to office at her own time, whereas Atsi was working in a private school as an English teacher. She was a dedicated teacher. In their off time, they were always together on their toes roaming, going for shopping or gossiping with friends or going to farmhouse. Whenever Atila came to talk to me, we used to wish each other cheerfully to start gossiping, which ultimately turned into quarrels very often. We enjoyed teasing or irritating each other. She was not at all ready to tolerate any adverse comments about Kiphire. She loved her native land more than she loved herself.

In case of a bit strong wind, if I happened to catch her any place I used to tell her, "Oh! You are a brave lady."

"Thank you," she used to respond delightedly but smelling something odd she used to enquire, "But, why? Ki hoisey?…Kobina? What's happened?"

"See the wind is so strong. It can easily blow your thin body to near your office. Even then you …"

She started laughing in anger, "Hochha? Mar khabo de! (Is it? I will beat you!)." She started running behind me furiously.

She was very frank to me. I never questioned her about anything personal but she revealed that she was in love with a person from Tuensang who was a Professor by profession. She very often talked about him and she used to go to Tuensang to her lover. It was indeed true love from her side. She had so many dreams for their future life and family. She wanted to have happy life with him. Very often, she used to spend her vacation or weekends with him. She looked so happy after coming back from Tuensang. Her marriage with that man seemed just a matter of time.

But unfortunately after few months some cursed shadow pervaded their relation. That time Atila came hurt. After a few days she stated that her lover was not ready to get married at that time. She was crying. She disclosed that she was conceiving. I did not want to know about her reaction against such deception by that man but I was eager to know about her decision about the life she was hosting in her womb.

Atila said that she would not go for abortion or discard the child. She was adamant. She stated, "I am a working woman. Even if I am not, then also I don't care. I would have searched for a work for the sake of the child. But I am definitely going to give birth to the child."

I saluted her in my mind. I said, "You are a brave lady! Really … hochha. I am serious." We laughed a lot.

Her family, her father, mother, sister and relatives, came in her support. Nobody discouraged her nor put her under unnecessary and irritating questionnaires. There was no hush-hush either in their house or among neighbours. Her mother was so happy that Atila took a wise decision.

Her father said, "I am proud of my daughter. Her indulging in relationship with that man may be merely a mistake or wrong on her part, but discarding the child would have been a sin and an act of cowardice."

I only told Atila, "I think our ultimate aim is to be happy, to be content and it is our duty rather to keep ourselves happy. But we should all know that everybody can't get everything, he or she wants here under the sky. We must learn to be happy whatever we have at our hand, at our reach and that is real art of living. Reason behind being happy may be very less than that of being sorry but those less causes for happiness are always stronger than those numerous causes of becoming unhappy. We are stronger when we are happy."

Atila started smiling, "Is not it heavy?"

"What?"

"That what you are saying," she was still smiling, "Are you a sort of disciple of any sage?"

"Oh! Yes, I am a disciple of nature. I always try to learn from the natural being around me. See the wild herbs, with its unknown little flower, are as happy as the well-nourished rose with its voluptuous bloom in our garden or room. They are never worried about not getting whatever does not come in their way."

She seemed consented, "Hoi to. Hocha achhey de. It is very true. I am happy that I am no more in dilemma and I can live independently, but I need not to think to opt to be sad as I have all support of my family. I am really very lucky, see."

She continued, "You know, now I don't care whether I have been deceived by any one or not but I know I have not cheated myself or my conscience. I indulged in a true love, a selfless love. Now I believe love is not greater than life. Life can make love stay alive. I hope I will be able to find throbbing in my child to love life by forgetting all forgettable."

I found her sobbing in her heart. I asked her, "So, Malik comes in the forgettable category?" She started smiling, "Mar khabode".

I said, "You know you look very pretty while smiling. When we smile, we make the grief to get afraid of us. We never know what will be there for us next day. The basic of living is actually not allowing any sense of dying to come there in mind. Above all, time is the best consumer."

So after a few days, Atila left for Kohima for a long vacation. Her parents said that she was in need of proper looking after and medical care. It was a long parting for us.

And then when one morning I was getting amazed, as usual, looking at the orchids, I was fostering in my terrace, I got the happy news from Atila's father that she gave birth to a child previous evening. Atila became mother of a lovely son and both were well.

After almost one month, Atila came back to Kiphire with her most adorable son. The moment he opened his eyes he conquered all of us and defeated, and drove away, all sorts of gloom. The whole town became concerned for the wellbeing of the child. We used to be eager to hear his intelligible vocals.

Children or infants really come with all divine grace to make everybody and everything around delighted. They make everybody pleased by their glance. Their uttering any sound makes us gape by forgetting everything else. We make ourselves lean before them with all sincere submission for their little touch. We find all reason to be happy by overlooking all agony when we are with them.

That child enabled Atila to rejuvenate once again with the same zeal. I found her to smile, to laugh, to work like ever before. She really got the spirit again to create a new world for herself, full of all most all known people, and to live lively in that world after becoming the mother of that child.

Her parents arranged the naming ceremony in a grand way. All the neighbours and their relatives assembled that day in their house. It was a great show of solidarity and support to Atila to lead her life looking ahead, and such esteemed support could be possible only in a strong society. We were invited to witness the ceremony. All took part in the prayer for blessing of God for the child and wished a long and happy life for him and the mother. None talked anything about the man who deceived Atila. It was exemplary for all others and for every society.

37.   Being in Limbo in Between Life and Death

It was another dark morning full of fog and mist. I came to Kiphire NST bus stand. It was a chilling cold of December but I was to go down to Kohima to our headquarters. The Nagaland State Transport bus was ready to move, at least the driver and the conductor were posing that they will be leaving at any moment, but actually, the driver was blowing the horn to attract some more passengers as there were only a few people there that day to go to the Kohima side. The road was wet like any other rainy day. So, most of those few passengers were enjoying hot tea.

Meanwhile the driver kept on playing the horn but failed to bring any more passengers. So only 16-17 passengers ultimately boarded and bus started moving. I wrapped myself with a Naga-shawl on all my warm clothes to safe my ears from cold. My ears and foot were found to be too sensitive to bear with low temperature. I was seating on a window seat just behind the space of the conductor.

"Kot jabo saab? Where are you going?" asked the middle aged man who seated beside me. We knew each other by our face.

"I am going to Kohima. Kohima jaboley ache de. Apuni?"

He was also going to Kohima. We started talking about the weather, the crops, roads, Christmas and about many other things. As usual, the driver stopped the bus at police points, at hospital stands and then at Kiphire village gate and got a few passengers. It was most unfortunate for me that I was seating at window seat but could not enjoy watching outside due to the black screen of fog and mist. So after the bus covered the first lap downwards after crossing Kiphire village I preferred to let my sight in rest closing my eyes and to listen all co-passengers discussing various important and unimportant arguments. They were talking and laughing loudly. The bus was going on a good speed on that spiral road downward the slope of the hill on the top which Kiphire village was located.

All of a sudden, there was a massive jerking with huge sound, as if the tyre of our bus or something had blasted near my eyes. Before I could guess anything, an extreme thrust blew my body to the backside of the seat in front of me. For the fraction of a moment, I could see the bus roll downwards and the inner surface of the roof of the bus was under my feet. I was again thrown to another direction and everything became black and dumb before my eyes. I was no more there in that very time of that very horrible event.

I got my sense back for a brief time after about three days in Kiphire Hospital. There was extreme drowsiness and pain throughout my body. Extreme pain was there in my head, in my ribs, hands, back and in my legs. I found the world fully hazy and dim when I tried to open my eyes. The light in the room hurt my eyes the most. I supposed I found myself a stranger in that indistinct surrounding full of inarticulate noise. I could not make out what was happening with me or so with others there. My eyes failed to bear with the light and eyelids were closed again.

But somehow my soul resumed living from that very moment after a break. I discovered that life, certainly nothing but a sense riding on ether, venturing all cells of my body, its kingdom. Life was nothing but an imperceptible centre, pivoting every aspect of my being alive, at that moment that was being greeted with enormous pain from every cell of mine. I also discovered that the pain all over my body sustaining the very sense of my being alive. Slowly I could differentiate voices around me, I could not see those faces but I could very well guess voices of Mandal, Lipong, Suraaj, Zezi, Das, Atila or Tsanio and all my friends who prayed day and night for me and all other who were hurt.

Then I was lost again in stupor and when I became able to open my eyes again, I found myself in the bed of Kohima Hospital and it was the face of my mother before my eyes. She and my brother reached Kohima that day. They were sobbing. I was not able to utter a single word.

The moment doctors at Kiphire Hospital and Dr. Singh of our department got positive responses from a corporeal me, and found me to be out of coma-phase, I was shifted to Kohima Hospital. It was a deadly accident. The driver failed to turn properly at a U-bend just down below Kiphire village and dashed the hill directly. The strike made the bus to get thrown out of the road and roll down along the slope of the hill, to the bed of the Zinky river, about 300-400 metres steep down from the road there, like a rolling stone, sometimes somersaulting in the air then again thrashing heavily on the hill. Out of 21 passengers, 11 ill-fated persons died on the spot, by being caged in that cursed bus which was finally knocked violently near the Zinky river and was shattered into pieces.

I survived mysteriously. My body was recovered from a groove of a rock a few feet down from the road. Immediate after the bus got its knock with the hill I might have gotten a heavy blow on the backside of my skull that caused me to be unconscious. I don't know how or who dragged or threw my body out of the bus in that crucial moment. Villagers immediately carried my body to Kiphire Hospital where I was kept under all possible intensive care. I received at least 13 stitches on my skull. It was selfless rescue operation by the people of Kiphire village and Assam Rifles Jawan that some passengers and I somehow survived.

The accident was in the news widely and it shocked all. It was either miscommunication or wrong interpretation that my family were not sure whether I was alive or not. After reaching Dimapur they came to know that life had not deserted my body. Hence, tear in the eyes of my mother, brother and all at that occasion was a normal phenomena. Not all blissful moments can be expressed by happy smile, there comes rare occasion that there left nothing but tears to express about ones happiness explicitly.

All my senior officers and colleagues rendered all support to me and my family members in Kohima. It was hard work of all my well-wishers and prayers for me in Kiphire and in Kohima that I resumed living. After about 4-5 days in Kohima Hospital, I started responding properly. Gradually I started walking for a few steps. I got one of my ribs severely damaged. My legs and hands were injured terribly. Skull was smashed. Doctors were afraid that my spinal cord was gravely hurt. I was not able to sit even for a few moments.

Through the window of my room in the hospital, I could see the glowing sun sometime. I wondered where my soul or sense would have been for those 3-4 days when I was in a coma. Why could I not recollect what happened to me or to the bus in that fatal moment? Who dragged me out of the bus? I heard much about the state of coma. State of 'coma' cannot be experienced. I cannot remember anything about the period in between the moment I found my world turned black, after the strike on my skull in the bus, and the moment I got back my sense and opened my eyes in Kiphire Hospital. Then I cannot recall anything about my journey from Kiphire to Kohima. For me it was really an illusion that I found myself lying on the bed of Kohima Hospital and my mother sobbing before me. Perhaps my pulse was on, I was not responding but I was not sleeping or dreaming. I was surprised what the state it was actually which I passed through. How came those days got deleted from my memories? My life-span is actually the life other than those three days. I found our body to be the abode of the soul, which is actually nothing but a shadow of the incorporeal Almighty, whereabouts of whom none can explain. The soul leaves this body in some occasions, as in my case, for some unknown place from where it may or may not return.

Why I was judged to live again? I supposed my soul travelled up to near the sun where God might have his court, during those days of absence of my soul in my corporeal being. There He must have found that a lot more work yet to be done by me on the earth. So they consider my soul to get back again into my body so that I can complete all those pending work. From that bed, I tried to talk to the ultimate disposer. I know He knows that I love this world. I love to live. I don't want to miss this world, its sky, soil, silence, noise, radiance or darkness.

I was released from Kohima Hospital after a few days for further treatment at my home place. I travelled all the way from Kohima to my home, even with my fractured body, in ease as I was in a near stupor since I was spared under influence of some soporific. So when I came back in sense again I found myself at my home among my family and friends.

One Neurologist, as well as one Orthopaedic specialist kept me under comprehensive medical care. After a thorough examination, it was found that I actually had some major injuries in my spinal cord. The dorsal '8'&'9' and limber spines '2'&'3' were found to receive some hairline-fractures. So I was suggested to be in a complete bed rest for months which appeared to be a bitter punishment for me. My body and every muscle, not accustomed with such a long rest, revolted badly. It was aching all over my body to make me to suffer a lot. It pained me to the deepest to be lying on bed for all most 24 hours a day.

I was compelled to talk and to repeat a lot on the accident, about Nagaland and about people of Nagaland to all who came to visit me. All saluted people there in Nagaland as they realised that it was the selfless support of those wiser people in Nagaland that I was able to return to my home. Talking about Nagaland, and about people there, used to give me immense pleasure.

After a few days, I was given a synthetic or metal belt for whole of my back, from neck to waist, to support my waist and spine in case of my leaving bed for even some minutes. Gradually I started walking some steps without any help and then it was fast coming back of mine to the course of life. Soon I could walk a good distance. After about two months, I found myself able to move around with that belt on my back. That very belt became part of my body and remained so nearly for next two years.

I was happy that I got the opportunity to remain among my family for so long at a stress. It never happened before that I was allowed any leave for more than 15 or 20 days from my office, at a stress, to remain at my native. But at the same time I was missing Kiphire and my friends there. So days ran fast and after about three months, I was again to proceed from my home to the home, away from home, in Nagaland among all-round green. That time I was not alone, the body-hugging belt on my back was with me at my every step. After reaching Kohima I realised that I was no more in ease to roam around or to climb up even a few steps. I could manage to walk slowly for a fair distance on a flat or fair slope. It was very difficult for me to sit on chair for even a few minutes at a stress as I used to feel an acute pain at my lower back, for weight of my upper portion of my body wholly came on the damaged portion on my spinal cord, I supposed, while seating on the chair. But I knew that agility was the best medicine for all such physical adversity.

After a few days, I came to Kiphire again. Friends in Kiphire received me with warm and heartily greetings. They were so glad to see me back at Kiphire and walking freely. Zezi jumped on me and held me tight in joy, that I was back alive. Atila cheered like Tarzan. But life turned different for me. I could hardly climb any height, I could not have exercise or outdoor games, I could not run or hop. I was not even able to bent a bit or walk fast. I was afraid that the world would pass fast.

But it did not happen as people came in my support. They kept on enquiring about my health, or whether I was facing any problem. All prayed to the Almighty for me. Christians came with blessings from the church, Muslims bought a lot of 'Dua' and Hindus came with 'Prasada' or wishing boon from heaven.

Then once I came to visit the spot of that horrific accident that made many to lose their lives and me to be deprived of agility. I was baffled to see the seemingly innocent looking U-turn on the road there. But when

I turned to the other side of the road open to the steep downwards ravine ended at the bed of the river Zinky it made me to shiver as a sense like icy cool wave all over my body. It was so steep that I could guess that there was simply no chance for that bus to stop rolling once it rolled down from the road after hitting the hill. It was terrible to find the skeleton of that cursed bus still on the bed of the river from that point of the road. I was shocked, and at the same time I was surprised as to how I survived! That wreckage of the bus was hosting some wild bushes there near the river. I found my eyes to host some wild tears. I wanted to go down to that wreckage, but I could not go down so steep at that time.

Within a few days, when I came to Kohima at our head-office for some official work I was told that I had been considered for transfer to my home state on health ground. So I got hardly any time after that to spend at Kiphire or in Nagaland. Everything happened so fast. I left Kohima behind, I left Dimapur behind and I left Guwahati behind. But those were partings for merely my corporeal being as my mental attachment with Nagaland was, and is, unending. For every reason my mind roams all those places at Kiphire or in Kohima and dug out the inspiration. I will always be in debt to those people of Nagaland, a land with perpetual treasure.